MELISSA FORD THORNTON

ECLIPSES:
BEHIND THE BORDERLINE
PERSONALITY DISORDER

☾

MONTE SANO PUBLISHING

> The information provided in this book is to be used for informational purposes only. It should not be used as a substitute for seeking *professional* diagnosis, treatment, and care.

Quantity discounts are available. For more information please write to:
Monte Sano Publishing, PO Box 824, Madison, AL 35758
or call:1-800-508-9461 (US/Canada) or 256-922-9963.

World Wide Web: http://www.msano.com

FIRST EDITION

Book design and cover by Marcia Hoppers

Publisher's Cataloging–in–Publication
Thornton, Melissa Ford.
     Eclipses : behind the borderline personality disorder / Melissa Ford Thornton. – 1st ed.
     p. cm.
     Includes bibliographical references and index.
     ISBN: 0–9659392–2–7
     1. Borderline personality disorder–Popular works. 2. Borderline personality disorder–Treatment. 3. Behavior therapy.
     I. Title.
RC569.5.B671997   616.85'852
                                   QBI97–41052

This book is printed on acid–free paper.
Printed in the United States of America.
10 9 8 7 6 5 4

For my husband, Mark, more loving and loved
than mere words can express.

ACKNOWLEDGMENTS

I hold deep gratitude for more people than I can
list. I pray you know who you are. I wish to thank my
publisher, Marcia Hoppers, for her insight and
professionalism. Drs. William Barley, Alice Chenault,
and Eric Peterson for their professional knowledge and
editing; the anonymous people who speak out in this book
and make it what it is—a strong message of encourage-
ment from one who is making it to one who is struggling
to do so; my family—the Fords and the Thorntons—
who supported me collectively and individually all the
way; to the following mental health professionals who
did their work with warmth and compassion: Psychiatric
Aides—especially "St. Peter, St. Paul" and Benji, nurses,
and recreational therapists. To all those who believed in
me and in the reality of this book. Finally, to my mother,
Suzanne Bourne Ford, who succumbed to depression, but
who lived a richly textured life joyfully and fully—
teaching me even now to never give in to dark feelings
and inevitable tragedies and bumps in life. She would
say: "Know the sun always shines behind the moon in an
eclipse. Soon it will shine on you."

ABOUT THE TITLE

(Solar) **eclipse** *noun:* (1) the obscuration of the light of the sun by the moon (2) a reduction or loss of splendor, status, etc.

The title of this book depicts the feeling of darkness that shuts out the light of hope when the mind becomes afflicted. Hope and light are not lost, only hidden behind layers of dark emotions that have clawed their way to the forefront of the consciousness. Hope is never lost. The sun will shine again—if you give life a chance.

NOTE ON PSEUDONYMS

Pseudonyms have been used for the borderline patients who have chosen bravely to share their stories in this book, to protect their privacy. Some of my experiences with the disorder are indicated by my initials, *MFT.*

TABLE OF CONTENTS

ACKNOWLEDGMENTS III
ABOUT THE TITLE/NOTE ON PSEUDONYMS IV
FOREWORD VII
INTRODUCTION 1
Chapter 1
   A SLUMBER PARTY 5
Chapter 2
   DIAGNOSIS: EMOTIONALITY OR REALITY...OR BOTH? 15
Chapter 3
   INPATIENT HOSPITALIZATION 32
Chapter 4
   DRAWBACKS TO LONGER TERM CARE 61
Chapter 5
   DIALECTICAL BEHAVIOR THERAPY (DBT) 68
Chapter 6
   USING ALL THE TRICKS OF THE TRADE 87
Chapter 7
   TREATMENTS 102
Chapter 8
   FAMILY RELATIONSHIPS 112
Chapter 9
   RECOVERY: THE HELL OF GETTING WELL 119
Appendix A
   A WORD ON THE REPRESSION RAGE 128
Appendix B
   FAREWELL TO HIGHLAND 131
Appendix C
   WHERE ARE ALL THE BOYS? 133
DIAGNOSTIC CRITERIA 134
GLOSSARY 135
NOTES 139
BIBLIOGRAPHY 140
WHO TO CONTACT FOR MORE INFORMATION 141
INDEX 144

☾ FOREWORD

We see the author of *Eclipses: Behind the Borderline Personality Disorder*, Melissa Thornton, as a remarkable woman. Her book is different and needed in that it describes personal experiences of someone identified as "borderline," who tells the reader very clearly what the disorder feels like as it is being experienced, i.e., like being in hell. *Eclipses* is a unique book not only about the reality of the author's illness and experience with institutionalization, but also about a life-saving treatment for a psychiatric illness formerly thought to be intractable. It is not written from a clinician's view but from a patient's view. This increases everyone's understanding of the disorder—fellow borderlines, their families and clinicians. For all of us, this is an invaluable insight. The book is clear, concise, and down-to-earth.

Melissa Thornton is not one of "the worried well." She is not "hysterical." She also is not bothersome, bad, manipulative, or any of the other things often attributed to people with borderline personality.

(Even today, some therapists refuse to take a patient with borderline personality disorder into their practice, mainly based on the "old school" thoughts of them as manipulative, "bad" people. Some view them as too manipulative to be worthy of or successful in therapy. Some feel they are more suited to an institution—even criminal institutionalization. Other therapists feel they simply can't manage the erratic, draining, dependent behaviors of borderline patients in the throes of their most intense suffering.)

We see this author for who she is—one of a large number of people with this disorder, estimated to be between 1.8% and 4% of the U.S. population—literally millions of people, who have been profoundly damaged by their biology and certain of their life experiences, and who are trying their best to make a life worth living while striving to get even better.

We like and respect this author, and we feel the same way about the others with this disorder who are anonymously described in the following pages. If we did not hold closely these beliefs and feelings, how could we work so hard to help them find a path toward a less painful life?

Treatment of borderline personality disorder varies. Many medications have been used, with some success, to treat various aspects of the disorder. Other kinds of psychosocial treatments have also been used. Yet, Melissa Thornton's treatment, Dialectical Behavior Therapy (DBT), is the only treatment that has been tested in randomized clinical trials and found superior to "treatment as usual in the community."

DBT's superiority has been seen in terms of fewer and less severe self-harm behaviors, a higher rate of staying in treatment, fewer emergency room visits and psychiatric hospitalizations, reduction of angry feelings, better, sometimes faster social adjustment, and the decreased use of certain medications.

So far, the research indicates that DBT changes very important behaviors in life-saving and life-enhancing directions. However, it is important to remember that up to 10% of the people with this disorder ultimately commit suicide.

Psychologist Marsha Linehan, Ph.D., of the University of Washington, Seattle, developed this behavior therapy. She is quick to acknowledge that we must have a better treatment, one that can ease emotional distress better than anything we have now. However, that does not negate the fact that DBT already has saved and enhanced lives.

DBT is not simply a suicide-prevention program, although it is partially that. It is more emphatically a concerted, collaborative effort between patient and psychotherapist to improve the quality of the person's life, to develop a way for the borderline patient to see life as worth living—no matter how painful at times.

Hearteningly, the course of the borderline personality disorder is one of improvement as the years pass. By some point in the middle years, up to 75% of people with this disorder will no longer meet the diagnostic criteria for it. Therefore, enhancing their lives in the meantime is imperative. If our patients will stay alive, they have a very good chance of getting significantly better. DBT is one way of attaining this result.

As a clinical psychologist and a psychiatrist, respectively, we value what this treatment does for us and for our patients. Dr. Linehan saw a need for both a compassionate approach and a pragmatic system that supports the psychotherapist. DBT helps therapists maintain their interest in and energy for what can be at times the difficult task of helping borderline sufferers stay safe, have reasons for getting up every morning, and keep going.

DBT balances acceptance of the patient as she or he is with ceaseless teaching and strengthening of concrete ways of tolerating and solving problems. It encourages respect for troubled people who are our fellow human beings and who are doing the best that they can each moment to deal with desperate feelings and, sometimes the full-time job of staying alive.

DBT encourages incremental, tolerable changes in behavior. It helps psychotherapists to observe their own limits and to be their most humane selves. When this happens, they are less likely to drive their patients away or to be driven away by them, possibilities the "old school" approaches and attitudes indicate are all too common.

In fact, DBT dramatically enhanced the quality of our lives as therapists. We experience more "intrusions" into our private lives, as DBT practitioners. But, far from feeling increasing frustration and burnout, it has improved our relationships with our suffering patients and alleviated the aggravation that once sapped much of our energy.

We have a clarity of purpose and an ability to recognize and appreciate the constructive efforts and successes of people like Melissa Thornton, who today is capable of writing a unique, touching, informative book about her illness and therapy. As clinicians, we need more feedback from patients who can give us the borderline point-of-view. Seeing success allows us to be of much greater service to other Melissas.

Hats off to the author and others portrayed in what you are about to read. It is a valuable, unique blend of the personal and the medical. We are grateful to participate in this new view of what helps many desperate people. It pushes us to work with even more fervent commitment to our profession.

William D. Barley, Ph.D.
Eric W. Peterson, M.D.

Asheville, North Carolina

❨ INTRODUCTION

You're going along fine, and suddenly *Wham!* You've hit a brick wall and there's nowhere to run, no one to understand. You scream, tear out your hair, take over-the-counter sleeping pills to calm down enough to stop crying at night. The next day, you get up, sluggishly. You go to work and get the job done. You might even fake a smile every now and then to keep up the facade to show there is no brick wall in your life. You're okay. You're like everybody else. But, you're not. The darkness is back. It has eclipsed your happiness, shaken your confidence, rocked your very nerve endings. Who can you tell about this? Why don't the lights work when you've been eclipsed? You are alone in the dark and you are afraid the sun might never shine again.

You suffer from borderline personality disorder (BPD). Ironically, you are too afraid to seek the very help that could lead you to the hope-filled road of recovery. Instead, you hurt inside, so you begin to hurt yourself outside to match those powerful hidden emotions, or to punish yourself for something you feel should receive punishment, or to get temporary relief from the awful feelings assailing you, or for many other reasons therapists can help ferret out—but only if you ask for help.

Yeah, make your arm bleed, bang your forehead on the headboard, harder, *harder!* Scream at those you love until, they slink off, terrified of you, the traitors! Burn your fingers on the stove, prick your hand with a pin over and over and *over.* Take those pills. Buy more, stock up, this might just be the *big eclipse.*

Scary? The world of the borderline is a scary place, where logic as most people know it, is eclipsed. It is a place where emotions rage wildly, often with self-harmful, if not fatal, consequences. It's a place where there are only black or white answers, where people are either good or bad, where something that happens is wonderful or so horrible it seems an hysterical, emotional response is appropriate. Or, worse, it seems that whatever is so terrible is their fault. They, those other people, are the evil culprits because they aren't good enough; they aren't perfect. If they are evil, then they deserve to be punished. That's often when the self-harm begins. It's not, however, when it stops. The punitive behavior becomes habitual, a pattern, for the borderline. This behavior is as painful, literally, as living life on the edge of a razor blade…and it can kill.

Before this illness, I had never been hospitalized in a psychiatric ward. When I was diagnosed, I had two magazine articles, both dated, and one thin book *I Hate You–Don't Leave Me: Understanding the Borderline Personality*. As helpful as these materials were, they weren't enough. I longed to hear of other borderlines who had been helped and now had a life worth living. Where was some sort of practical guide about psychiatric hospitalization, beyond the introduction pamphlets for family members that were mostly filled with rules and regulations?

Although, my doctors answered all of my questions as thoroughly as possible, neither my husband nor I really knew what questions to ask. We were suddenly on another planet where the old logic no longer applied. We were terrified. Ironically, we were not alone. Psychiatrists estimate that 23 percent of all psychiatric inpatients and 11 percent of outpatients are diagnosed with borderline personality disorder. When I became an inpatient, I learned that some of my best allies were right next to me. They were fellow borderlines trying their best to get through each day— without a map or manual.

—MFT

This book does not offer the answers of a manual. It does, however, offer things from the borderline point of view. Of particular interest may be the information on Dialectical Behavior Therapy (DBT). This behavioral approach to the borderline diagnosis is producing promising results.

If you are hanging on by a fingernail, and need to read about success first—please read the introduction and then turn to "Testimonials" in Chapter 5. Although real situations of patients have been woven into the fabric of this book, straight talk about how some form of hospitalization and therapy, namely DBT, saves lives is concentrated in these two parts of the text. Perhaps reading it first, then taking in the other information more slowly might be best for you at this time. Always, do what is best for you. Be sure to seek professional help first—this book is meant to be a friend not a doctor.

Today, I am alive and living in my home writing about something that nearly claimed my life. But before I gained the skills and control to reach this place, I had to live in different settings and far from home. As radio star and author Garrison Keillor said, "I'm happy to be here."

—MFT

If you feel like you want to read success stories first, turn to "Testimonials" on page 69 in Chapter 5.

Chapter 1

◖ A SLUMBER PARTY

What a weekend! Kimberly's husband was going to be gone on U.S. Reserves duty, and she invited several of her friends to join her at her home for a sleep over. They brought chips and dip, rented movies (comedies) and all managed to squeeze—with an extra mattress on the floor—into one room and talk until one by one the four fell into peaceful sleep. Nobody had taken each others' threats of putting toothpaste in the ear of the first to fall asleep seriously.

Peggy and Isabelle had traveled the farthest to reach this playful rendezvous. They both lived in the same city and the trip was about five hours by car. Emily lived in a neighboring state, about forty minutes from Kim's. She often visited Kim, but the sleep over was something special. She even conjured up her Raggedy Ann doll for the occasion.

A high school reunion? A sorority alumna bash? No. These women, Peggy, Emily, Kimberly, and Isabelle share a bond that perhaps transcends sisterhood. They had been in the hospital where each was learning how

5

to survive. A psychiatric institution brought these women together, and their stories, while varied, share many common elements.

One thing these women share is the diagnosis of borderline personality disorder. This illness, in its most simplified description, is given to emotionally vulnerable, parasuicidal individuals. In clinical terms they are emotionally dysregulated. In other words they have difficulty controlling and tolerating their feelings and have hurt themselves. Their parasuicidal behavior must be taken seriously. Parasuicide is any unsuccessful suicide attempt.

"The essence of the disorder is a combination of first, an overly emotional temperament or inborn emotional style, second, invalidation of this temperamental problem by the family, and third, the adoption by the person of extreme self-destructive ways to cope with their extremely painful feelings," according to Marsha Linehan, Ph.D.

Vulnerability and invalidation feed off each other, worsening each as well as the situation for the individual. That is, the more vulnerable a person is, the more sensitive to invalidation they become; the more invalidating an environment, the more heightened their sensitivity becomes. Unfortunately, the third factor—maladaptive coping mechanisms transacts with the other two—creating an unbearable emotional world that, somehow, amazingly is borne by borderlines—or they end their pain by ending their lives. However, suicide only opens the floodgates of pain for those left behind.

Underlying these factors is the basic biological vulnerability that borderlines have from birth—a low emotional "immune system" that makes them predisposed to painful emotionality—either too much or too little and extreme difficulty in returning to a "normal" emotional state once their emotions have been triggered.

It is important to note that parasuicide is any non-fatal intentional act of self-harm, whether the conscious consequence was meant to be death or not. In fact, often intent is so difficult to distinguish that the term parasuicidal was developed to explain the difficulty in determining whether death was consciously desired. For instance, a person may overdose expecting to be found in time to be saved, but die by accident. Others may die in car "accidents" they carefully orchestrate.

Dr. Eric Peterson explains, "With BPD, generally self-harm involves the three R's: Relief, Rescue, and Revenge." For many borderlines, parasuicide becomes an automatic response to hurtful events or mishaps they encounter. And, at some level, they rely on the pattern of the three R's. Revenge is not necessarily an obvious motive, but once processed with an objective party, borderlines may come to see that it was the boss, the spouse, the mother-in-law, even the psychiatrist they hoped to lash back at for some deed done or undone.

For other borderlines, relief is all they seek. Dr. William Barley notes that only ten percent of those diagnosed with BPD actually end their lives in suicide. He explains that DBT doctrine upholds that relief is the predominant motive, which the therapist is encouraged to assume in the absence of evidence of another or other motive(s). The person's behavior is an understandable desire to escape or avoid emotional pain. In some cases, feelings of relief and revenge govern an individual's actions, which usually are more drastic and less habitual than those who hope, on some level of consciousness, to be found and rescued before they die from their behavior.

Although borderlines who seek one or two of the R's may see death as the only option, through Dialectical Behavior Therapy, new means of relief can be found. "DBT is a broad-based cognitive-behavioral treatment developed specifically for BPD. It was the first psychotherapy shown [in] controlled clinical trials to be effective with this disorder".[1] Marsha Linehan, Ph.D. developed specific DBT skills training that has been put in practice throughout the U.S. in an outpatient setting. However, Highland Hospital (see Appendix B) in Asheville, North Carolina and New York Hospital, Cornell Medical Center, Westchester Division (White Plains, New York) have been the first inpatient settings where DBT has been used to assist borderline patients.

Dr. William Barley emphasizes the importance of skills training for borderline patients and expands Linehan's quotation. He says, "DBT is the only treatment approach shown in a randomized clinical trial to decrease parasuicidal behavior in patients with borderline personality disorder".[2]

The first goal of DBT skills training is to eliminate parasuicide—this is extremely important if the patient is to move on to useful coping and change skills. As long as those with BPD remain a danger to themselves, their destructive behavior must take priority. This severely limits therapeutic focus. An early commitment to life is, perhaps, one of the single best indicators that a patient will be successful in using the full skills "package" available to them, and, therefore, is an indicator that DBT therapy will be effective for the borderline patient.

These new skills must be practiced to the point that they become a natural response to life's valleys. As Dr. Peterson puts it, "It may feel unnatural at first to grab an ice cube rather than a razor blade. In fact, it can feel as awkward as a corrected golf grip—but it saves lives." Dr. Barley adds, "DBT skills help bring relief from and tolerance to unpleasant emotions. Therefore, it's not just a system of learning to change uncomfortable emotions, but to tolerate them, saving lives and making them worth living."

The women at the slumber party all shared the structured program of Dialectical Behavior Therapy while they were hospitalized and each continues to practice dialectical behavioral skills. Emily and Isabelle were roommates at the hospital for a time on the BPD unit. This was during Isabelle's second stay at the hospital. Her first admission was successful in some ways but did not prevent her from further self-harm. Her return was "inevitable" in the eyes of doctors, nutritionists, and social workers on her case. Maybe two stays will be the magic number for Isabelle. For it was during this second stay that Isabelle was able to form allegiances with others. Perhaps it's worth noting how allegiances form in the unfamiliar maze of corridors and footpaths that make up the grounds not only of a psychiatric hospital but of BPD and the treatment applied.

At Highland Hospital, as in many hospitals, a regimented schedule is enforced through a series of privilege levels. I found that out the hard way—my first five minutes on the ward. I asked to use the bathroom and was escorted by a nurse who watched me the entire time. I looked around in horror at slimy soap bars and wet wash cloths on the floor. I had been told I would share the bath with the patient whose door connected to the room and would share half a bedroom with the other bathroom user. Suddenly, although I was usually calm when scared, a switch flipped and I was screaming at the top of my lungs: *"Pigs! Pigs! I won't live with pigs!"* For my outburst, a medical doctor assigned to assess my safety level, restricted me to the ward.

It was a lonely night. My roommate was offended by being proclaimed a pig. She was a seventeen-year-old woman who had a self-concept other than pig—rightly so. This offended roommate showed up just at lights out and grumbled a few words to my heart-felt apologies. The next night she requested a room change. I was left feeling even more remorseful about my behavior and rejected to boot.

—MFT

To the borderline, these feelings of remorse aren't just fleeting feelings; they are shrapnel exploding within the body, spreading searing pain to every nerve. Isabelle had a reaction similar to mine on the ward. She later said she felt as though she had committed the ultimate faux pas and would not be able to find a single merciful soul among the patients, nurses, doctors, or psychiatric aides (PAs) who worked the ward. Instead of bonding with someone with common symptoms or interests her first night, Isabelle felt she had tainted her entire hospitalization. And, since abandonment is one of the greatest fears borderlines share, this feeling of aloneness just compounded her symptoms.

Enter Emily. She'd been in several hospitals without a definitive diagnosis. She's cynical and outspoken, but possesses the rarest of qualities: the ability to laugh at herself. Emily and Isabelle shared a room. Unlike my experience, Isabelle began to feel a connection. Even when the night shift male staffer entered their room demanding Emily's hair spray, Emily held her own. She didn't know it was a rule to have all "sharps" (objects considered potentially dangerous and kept locked in the nurses' station—sharp or not) turned in dutifully by 10 p.m. Emily laughingly said, "Oh yeah, I'm gonna spray myself to death," and dissolved into a series of giggles.

Isabelle laughed, even though she was afraid of the consequences. She tried to tell Emily that her privileges would be taken away, but the cavalier attitude reigned supreme. The next thing the women knew, two psychiatric aides were standing outside their door. One informed Emily that she would be restricted to the ward for 24 hours. Undaunted, Emily said, "Come in here and say that to me." The fellow bit the bait and in he came. Emily continued, "Is that other fellow making you do his dirty work? Make *him* tell me!" She played them like wild jokers, and Isabelle was impressed, scared, amused, and curious about her new roommate. Left alone at last, (with the exception of fifteen minute checks conducted by the night staff with flashlights) the two laughed into their pillows until sleep or suffocation threatened. They both rose early to grab what warm water might be left to them before doctor's rounds. Isabelle and Emily were finding a basis for friendship. But, they are only two of the sleep over participants.

These women bear scars. Some are on the outside where they have used matches, lighters, or sharp objects, such as razor blades, knives, or glass to slit their wrists or just hurt themselves, cut their flesh, or, as Isabelle once put it, "to see the blood and realize I'm not already dead." But these are just the scars we can see. They all have scars on the inside that are hidden and hard to heal. Histories of abuse, unhappy childhoods, non-supportive families, the loss of children, death of loved ones, these and more contribute to the depression and BPD with which sufferers are diagnosed.

Linehan writes, "that up to 75 percent of individuals with BPD have experienced some sort of sexual abuse in childhood. Histories of abuse seem to distinguish borderline individuals from other outpatient diagnostic groups."[3] Kimberly, Peggy, Emily and Isabelle share this shattering experience.

We invite you into the lives of these women and others. Although their names have been changed to protect their identities, their stories, which are the fabric, the heart, and soul of this book, are true life experiences. Yes, there is sadness in this book. But, life is not one big happy slumber party. The fact that these women could enjoy such a playful experience and fall asleep with an unfamiliar but welcome sense of peace is a tribute to the hope this book, Dialectical Behavior Therapy, and other interventions offer.

Dialectical Behavior Therapy is not a cure. Rather, as Dr. Barley says, "It is a new set of coping skills for those with BPD to use." He puts it quite frankly, "These are skills that will help keep you alive and have a life worth living until you feel better."

SUMMARY

∾ *Individuals with borderline personality disorder have difficulty controlling and tolerating their emotions.*

∾ *The borderline individual may have tendencies towards self-harm and may be suicidal.*

∾ *Ten percent of borderlines commit suicide.*

∾ *75 percent of borderlines were sexually abused as children.*

∾ *Abandonment is one of the greatest fears borderlines face.*

∾ *Dialectical Behavior Therapy teaches new skills to replace the self-destructive coping mechanisms borderlines develop "just to get by".*

Remnants of a Childhood

I return to a familiar sea
And retrace tiny footprints on the shore
That were erased by the incessant tide
So many years before.

Remnants of a childhood washing,
Like my sandcastles, out to sea
Setting sun casting shadows of
The child I used to be.

Sitting alone and clutching at
The sandy grains of time
I listen to the ocean waves
Whisper a forgotten nursery rhyme.

Remnants of a childhood washing,
Like my sandcastles, out to sea
Setting sun casting shadows of
The child I used to be.

Salty pools left on the beach
By a careless sea
Reflect grown-up eyes that
Can't understand these
Remnants of childhood still haunting me.

Melissa Ford Thornton
June 14, 1979
Hermosa Beach, California

Chapter 2

❰ DIAGNOSIS:
EMOTIONALITY OR REALITY...OR BOTH?

As long as she can remember, Isabelle has been prone to crying spells and a painful sense of loss which she could never identify except as a sharp feeling in her heart—so real it would make her want to choke. One of her brothers used to call her his "melancholy baby"— perhaps an interesting external impression of the BPD patient. Isabelle's mother noticed her child's extreme sensitivity at a fairly early age. She spoke to Isabelle about it, saying "You will feel life's hardships with more pain than other people. But, because you are extra sensitive you also have the capacity to feel life's joys more abundantly than others. That's the gift that comes with the price tag of sadness."

Initial Symptoms

Isabelle's mother had a poetic way of looking at the borderline personality. Certainly it applies to people who are emotionally vulnerable. The "gift of joy" that Isabelle's mother referred to, is another way of examining the basic outlook of those suffering from BPD. Those sufferers split things into simple, polemic pairs of good or bad, sadness or joy, black or white. Unable to grasp that something might be both good and bad, a person with BPD can only see the ends of the spectrum.

For example, a career can be a good thing. It brings in money, can add to a person's confidence in handling projects and people, it can provide satisfaction and fulfillment, give one a sense of purpose. Conversely, a career can add a lot of stress to a person's life—both on the job and at home. How often have you heard a working mother complain that her forty-hour a week job really requires more hours; that she already feels it takes her away from her children longer than she would prefer? How often have you heard stories of managers who sometimes take credit for their employees' projects? You've probably also heard of more and more companies cutting back on health and other benefits and placing more emphasis on productivity which leaves some employees feeling like a number rather than a person. These things feel "bad." So, a career can be seen as good or bad...or can both be true?

In her book *Girl, Interrupted* author Susanna Kaysen, once diagnosed as borderline, gives an eloquent account of this type of black and white thinking as she describes an outing she was allowed to take with other patients and nurses from McLean Hospital:

"The floor of the ice cream parlor bothered me. It was black-and-white checkerboard tile, bigger than supermarket checkerboard. If I looked only at a white square, I would be all right, but it was hard to ignore the black squares that surrounded the white ones. The contrast got under my skin. I always felt itchy in the ice cream parlor. The floor meant Yes, No, This, That, Up, Down, Day, Night—all the indecisions and opposites that were bad enough in life without having them spelled out for you on the floor."

For those with BPD, splitting things into these polemic categories is the only way they can encompass the reality of grey in their lives. Put another way, non-dialectical, imbalanced, one-sided thinking results from emotional vulnerability and invalidation and this combination worsens emotional dysregulation.

When Dr. Peterson tries to explain this type of "splitting", he often uses the model of a young emotionally vulnerable child who associates her mother with good. Mother provides food, sings lullabies, and hugs the child when she is frightened in the night. But, what if one day the child arrives home from kindergarten and finds an abusive mother? This mother ties up and beats the child rather than playing tea party. Or, the mother simply disappoints the child, by breaking a promise to go to the park because it rains that day or a similar disappointment. At such an early age, this child with the low emotional "immune system" cannot understand that mother is good in some ways and has problems in other ways which make her act badly toward the child. Much less can that child grasp the concept that mother cannot always do what the child wants or expects. So, the child "splits" the person: mother is good when she plays tea party. Mother is bad when she disappoints the child.

Later, an employer will be good when they praise this employee's work and bad when they criticize a proposal the employee writes. It has been said that shades of grey are invisible or nonexistent to the borderline. However, Linehan asserts that borderline patients cannot hold *both* black and white in their minds simultaneously. The more subtle shades might be possible, but like author Susanna Kaysen's vivid ice cream parlor metaphor, borderlines get by if they stare at the white square or stare at the black square—keeping good and bad in separate places in the brain and in life.

> *Borderline patients do not see both sides of the coin at once—we cannot hold two conflicting ideas in our minds at the same time. Yet, we must pull away from sheer darkness to feel lightness, from excruciating pain to feel some comfort; from suicidal intentions to a will to live. We must find that we can live in the rainbow of colors that exists between black and white thinking.*

Major Events

Therapists often have to work with a patient for some time to determine the major event or events that took place in this person's life that causes them to split. It's poignant that Isabelle's mother, who could so accurately speak to her daughter's sensitivity is the same person who took a lethal overdose of her medication and died in the living room of the home Isabelle had lived in as long as she can remember. This major event took place when Isabelle was 30 years old and happily employed.

Working from there, therapists discovered that Isabelle's mother was overweight most of her life and was verbally abused by Isabelle's father every evening at the dinner table. Isabelle wanted to be perfect; therefore she wanted to be the opposite of the mother she loved. At the time of her initial therapy, Isabelle weighed 70 pounds, which at 5 foot 1 inch placed her in physical danger from anemia, imbalanced electrolytes, and other symptoms of anorexia nervosa. Isabelle had never been fat. It puzzled doctors who worked with her, until they were able to learn, through intense therapy in a hospital setting, that the young woman firmly believed that she and her father had "killed" her mother. Obviously this was a distortion of Isabelle's thinking.

But, Isabelle did not see that. She felt she and her father were in a conspiracy of secrecy that ended in her mother's death. Isabelle's father had molested her when she was a child, a major event she repressed to the point of remembering only "a happy childhood with 'good' parents" (splitting). Isabelle's mother knew of the abuse, another fact Isabelle successfully repressed. Thus, without recalling these horrible events—except for her mother's suicide—Isabelle began starving herself, cutting her wrists, and overdosing on over-the-counter medication—attempting to take her own life.

She couldn't reconcile the kind and good mother with the one who wouldn't or couldn't protect her from her father's unwanted touch. Nor could she bring together the image of her father as the fun-loving, happy-go-lucky man she'd grown up believing in, with the father who made every meal a living hell for the family (especially his wife), cheated on his wife with several women, and molested his daughter. These were Isabelle's good parents; therefore, she, herself, must be bad. Before diagnosis and treatment, Isabelle unconsciously believed that the only way to find relief from these overwhelmingly intense emotions was to die. Her suicide attempts were almost successful. She was a high risk. She didn't want to live.

Dr. Linehan and others, such as Dr. Barley and Dr. Peterson, do not believe that abuse causes BPD, but, rather the invalidation of a vulnerable person lies at the source of this disorder. Significantly, in Isabelle's case there was most likely pre-existing emotional vulnerability.

Controversy over the validity of repressed memories currently rages within and without the psychiatric profession. For more detailed information on this, refer to Appendix A. Suffice it to say here that Isabelle's inability to recall early traumas has been diagnosed as post traumatic stress disorder and dissociative disorder. She left her body, successfully dissociating, or separating herself, from the events that caused her the most pain. She later remembered watching those same events the same way she watched her more current self-mutilation acts—with numbness, without physical pain. Dissociation creates this ability. It enables the mind to leave the body; often patients describe the experience as watching the events as if they were happening to someone in a movie. Or, they lack memory of an event because in their mind they weren't there at all; their minds had taken them somewhere else, somewhere safer, less terrifying.

Depending upon each individual, other initial symptoms of BPD might be depression, perfectionism, eating disorders, mood swings, self-destructive behavior, including the unintended destruction of healthy relationships such as marriages and friendships and the cultivation of potentially deadly behaviors such as drug, alcohol abuse, even numerous sexual encounters in this day of AIDS—all are symptoms of the borderline personality disorder. However, there are behaviors among some borderlines that may occur later. These include dropping out of therapy and escalating angry behavior to the point of needing restraints. But, these behaviors might not occur, especially with therapeutic care.

> *It's important to note that a person does not need to have all of the initial symptoms to be accurately diagnosed as borderline, nor do patients need to fear that they will develop the other symptoms over time.*

To help explain how each individual exhibits symptoms of BPD, take a look at the women at the slumber party. Peggy was severely depressed. She was consumed with trying to be a perfect wife and mother, yet as she watched the dissolution of her second marriage, she wondered why she seemed to be drawn always to the same type of man. But alcohol and drug abuse and casual sex were not part of her profile.

Kimberly suffered from immobilizing depression and drastic suicidal episodes. On the other hand, her deeply rooted belief in Christianity made her strive to adhere to traditional family values, but caused her tremendous conflict with the allure of suicide. Often she would say what so many potential suicides say when therapists or other patients ask: "What about your children? Can't you see they need you?" Kim's response was: "They'd be so much better off without me." Isabelle would call her on that. "My mom killed herself, and not a day goes by that I don't think about her and wonder what I did wrong. You think I'm better off?" Still Kim clung to her illusion of worthlessness to herself and others.

Some borderlines do not see their repeatedly bad choices in men and perfectionism as real problems. That is, they don't see it until they find themselves slightly depressed and alone one evening. They might drink an alcoholic beverage to relax and then do something as drastic as grabbing a large, serrated knife from the kitchen and stabbing themselves repeatedly. Not a superficial wound, such impulsive behavior can and often does require surgery.

Seeking Professional Help

Once a "garbage can" diagnosis for everything more serious than neuroses and less serious than psychoses, borderline personality disorder today is understood to be a serious disorder that *can* be treated. This is significant, since it once was a commonly held belief among psychiatrists that BPD would eventually lead to psychosis, i.e. schizophrenia, bipolar disorder (manic depressive disorder), or other psychotic disorders. We're stuck with this misleading name, "borderline", that does not sound serious. Because BPD causes so much pain for the individual, seeking professional care is of extreme importance.

Sadly and characteristically of borderlines, Isabelle waited a long time to seek professional help. As the book *I Hate You–Don't Leave Me* points out, borderlines function quite well in some types of careers and situations. Where there is structure, they excel. This is one reason it takes them a long time to recognize a problem, unless someone notes their more dangerous behavior and brings them to medical attention. Dr. Eric Peterson admits that this high functioning ability or "facade" is a frustration to many psychiatrists, himself included. He says, "Those with BPD often look composed, well groomed and present themselves in such an articulate manner that it seems their episodes of emotional outbursts, self-harm, irrational behavior is intentionally manipulative. I understand that is not the case, but I've worked with BP's for many years. Even today, someone can catch me off guard."

Isabelle, like many others with BPD, not only did not recognize the severity of her illness, but harbored emotions that prevented her from seeking help earlier. Her mother had been seeing a psychiatrist and she had killed herself. Isabelle thought psychiatrists were expensive quacks and that one, in particular, had killed her mother. She was splitting, again. Psychiatrists were bad and to be avoided. Yet, Isabelle desperately needed psychiatric help. She was young, intensely suicidal, and suffering from major depression before she timidly began the process of finding a psychiatrist who was "good."

But, once Isabelle, Kim, Peggy, and others or their families realize they need help, where can they turn? Mental health care is not something most people feel comfortable finding through the Yellow Pages. Although these listings can be helpful in limited ways. For example, some mental health professionals are listed under their areas of specialty. They might be marriage counselors, individual psychotherapists, or behavioral therapists.

Some distinctions might be helpful at this point. A psychiatrist has earned a medical degree and can prescribe medication. A psychologist usually, but not always, has earned a Ph.D. in some area of the mental health field and cannot prescribe medication. Psychotherapy is what Freud referred to as "talking therapy." This is what most people think of when they imagine a visit to a psychiatrist. Through discussing their problems and past and present experiences with an objective party trained in psychotherapy, patients with BPD can find some relief or coping mechanisms for their distress. On the other hand, behavioral therapy is aimed specifically at changing behaviors and often involves a series of steps and rewards. Someone who wants to quit smoking may seek out a psychiatric professional who will use behavioral therapy to gain their goal. Dialectical Behavior Therapy, obviously, is a behavioral therapy aimed first at stopping self-harmful acts and enhancing quality of life. However, it is a relatively new therapy and practiced by a small, but growing, number of clinicians. Therefore, although a casual perusal of the phone book can provide a variety of forms of mental health help, it is not likely to yield an expert in DBT. So much for the Yellow Pages.

So where do you turn next? Friends may have some excellent advice on mental health professionals in your area. You might find yourself amazed at the number of people you know who have, at one time or another, sought psychiatric help. Just as your friends could provide a worthwhile referral service for dentists, orthopedic surgeons, ob-gyns, and other specialists, they may know of mental health professionals. It is not something to be ashamed of, but unfortunately it appears to harbor some of its old stigma.

Understandably, you may not be ready to share your need with friends. Call your local Mental Health Association. They have a list of mental health professionals practicing in your area and are aware of their fields of expertise. Perhaps, the American Psychiatric Association (APA) can provide additional information on these professionals' qualifications. Research is your ally. You can make an appointment with a professional and ask about their background and qualifications. It is your right to interview them about these important points. Although most professionals charge for an initial session, some do not if you decide not to pursue treatment with them at that time. Perhaps someone has all the right credentials, but after your first few sessions with them, you don't feel you are in the right place.

Feel free to continue searching for a good match. Personalities are extremely important in psychiatry just as bedside manner is in other areas of medicine. Realize that your safety is paramount, and it might make sense to settle on some care, rather than hoping for a match made in heaven. BPD patients tend to be perfectionists by nature. This can be hazardous to your health in many ways, but especially if you continue to move from doctor to doctor as a way to escape or postpone care. Find someone you feel relatively comfortable with and begin therapy. Later, when you are more stable, you can change if you feel the need.

Don't expect your first session to be completely comfortable; you're stepping into unknown territory. And, don't expect to be "cured" after a few weeks of therapy. Give the professional and yourself the benefit of some time of working together before moving on. Most importantly, discuss any dissatisfaction with the professional and see if there can be an accommodation to your needs, before you move on too quickly. If the professional you're working with cannot meet your needs, they might be willing and able to give you an excellent recommendation of someone in their field who can. In fact, this is considered the most professional and mutually beneficial manner of switching therapists.

In some cases the original choice of a doctor may not be up to you. The previous information applies to outpatient counseling. This is all well and good if you recognize you have a problem, and subject yourself to psychiatric care. However, if you have a parasuicidal episode which lands you in the emergency room of a hospital, you may be asked to admit yourself voluntarily to the psychiatric unit of the hospital for further care. If you do not do this voluntarily, a family member or doctor can sign papers to have you committed.

This process is complex, and out of the scope of our focus on BPD. However, in general commitment involves appearance before a judge who will decide your ability to safely maintain yourself and/or not harm others. If you are found unsafe, you are placed in a state hospital (sometimes another type of hospital) for a period of time the state (not you, not your family) determines. It is in your best interest to keep your options open. Voluntarily admitting yourself gives you more choices.

If you are voluntarily admitted, a psychiatrist or other mental health professional may be assigned to you. If you have insurance or other means to pay, you can begin the "interviewing" process at this point. However, if you have no insurance or cannot pay, you may be assigned to a psychiatrist who works for the county on indigent cases. Your choices of doctors may be more limited in this case. But do *not* assume your care will be less satisfactory. If your doctor recommends inpatient treatment, you may be hospitalized for several weeks. One psychiatrist tells her patients to think of psychiatric hospitalizations in terms of weeks rather than days, largely due to the time it takes to make a diagnosis and try medications in a safe environment. Because some medications have serious side effects and others may prove ineffective for you, it may take a week or so to find the right one(s) and adjust the dosage. Psychiatric units do not normally handle specialized diagnoses such as BPD. In fact, a limited number of psychiatric hospitals in the United States have the professional experience to work successfully with BPD. The Westchester Division of New York Hospital's Cornell Medical Center in White Plains, NY has been implementing DBT into their program, almost from Dr. Linehan's inception of the therapy. However, Highland Hospital in Asheville, North Carolina is where our slumber party participants found a combined focus on DBT and psychodynamically oriented therapy, through individual and group counseling sessions. This combination proves significant. Linehan notes, "Stylistically, DBT blends a matter-of-fact, somewhat irreverent, and at times outrageous attitude about current and previous parasuicidal and other dysfunctional behaviors with therapist warmth, flexibility, responsiveness to the client, and strategic self-disclosure...".[1] This blending of fact-based logic with warmth and compassion is a powerful combination.

For example, Isabelle began learning skills that immediately decreased her suicidal actions. However, only through talking with an individual therapist over a period of months were members of her treatment team able to begin isolating the source of her anorexia, depression, and, at times, serious suicidal attempts. The abuse, dissociation, splitting, and serious desire to die were finally coming to light.

Emphasis on Validation

At Highland Hospital, these coping mechanisms were recognized, as such—a way of getting by. The aim of

Dialectical Behavior Therapy is to validate these mechanisms, no matter how maladjusted they may be, to nonetheless label them as unacceptable, and to replace them with healthy, safe coping skills. "The continuing efforts in DBT to 'reframe' suicidal and other dysfunctional behaviors as part of the client's learned problem-solving repertoire, and to focus therapy on active problem solving, are balanced by a corresponding emphasis on validating the client's current emotional, cognitive, and behavioral responses just as they are".[2]

To help explain how a maladjusted coping mechanism can be replaced with a safer one, remember Dr. Peterson's analogy of reaching for an ice cube in place of a razor blade. For serious "cutters" and others who cope by slashing themselves, this is a particularly effective DBT skill to employ. Holding ice cubes until they melt hurts. Your arm can feel literally as if it will fall off because it aches so much. This replacement skill provides the relief of self-inflicted pain many borderlines seek, without the tissue-damaging consequences of cutting or other drastic acts.

When working with borderline patients, Dr. Barley of Highland Hospital emphasizes the importance of validating the person and his or her coping skills. "These people are getting along the only way(s) they can. What they have been doing to this point is valid, if misdirected and ultimately not in their best interest. To tell someone with BPD 'you're screwed up, crazy to cut your wrists over someone else's expectations!' is about as damaging a thing a professional can do. Their reality is based on emotions. It is not our job to say 'that emotion is unreasonable—throw it out!' After all these patients have been through, further invalidation is the last thing they need from the psychiatric community or anywhere else. We don't ask our patients to look at their emotions or actions and deny them. We ask our patients to look at alternatives to these, and move forward."

Validation is extremely important for the borderline personality. Peggy's husband incessantly criticized her methods of child-rearing, indeed, her very personality. He wanted her to be active in the community while raising three young children. He wanted someone who would hang on his every word, praise his hard work at the office, and understand his interminably long hours spent there or at a local club "winning" over new clients. Peggy could not be all of these things. So, she fell into the trap her husband's behavior set for her. She invalidated herself: over and over again she told herself she was a failure at everything; she was no good; she was not a worthwhile human being. She became snappish with her children and began to question her ability as a parent, the one thing she thought she handled well. Severe depression overtook her, and she could no longer function in the world of invalidation where she now resided. She felt her only way out was to die.

Peggy recalls that her parents could be "pretty invalidating at times." She wanted to go into teaching as a career, and her father recited, "Those who *can,* do; those who *can't,* teach." To Peggy, his recitation invalidated her desire. But, she also remembers the first time her father ever said those precious words: "I love you." "I was in college, without money, without a car, and my parents were moving further away. I was so homesick I literally felt ill. I called them collect and that's when Dad said it. It meant the world to me."

Peggy recalls trying to please others continually for the crumb of the spoken words: "I love you." "I love to watch birds, especially in the winter when food is scarce, come to the feeder in my backyard. They are eating and getting by because I care and intentionally draw them to me by putting out food for them. In return, I am given the invaluable pleasure of watching their beauty and amazing skills of natural survival. These birds aren't living off of left-over crumbs. I assure you, it's not enough to live life off crumbs."

Peggy's second husband further broke down his wife's underlying structure of emotional vulnerability and validation with his constant treatment of her as a child. At every turn, Peggy remembers invalidating remarks and actions. Thus, her emotional vulnerability transacted with her invalidating environment. This combination was especially hard during an unintended pregnancy and after the birth of this surprise child, and Peggy's depression deepened to a dangerous level.

Linehan writes, "An invalidating family is problematic because…[it] leads to an intensification of the differences between an emotionally vulnerable child's private experience and the experience the social environment actually supports and responds to. Persistent discrepancies between a child's private experience and what others in the environment describe or respond to as her experience provide the fundamental learning environment necessary for many of the behavioral problems associated with BPD."

Further, "by punishing the expression of negative emotion" i.e. 'Go to your room and don't come out until you can put a smile on your face!' "and erratically reinforcing emotional communication only after escalation by the child, the family shapes an emotional expression style that vacillates between extreme inhibition and extreme disinhibition. In other words, the family's usual response to emotion cuts off the communicative function of ordinary emotions."[3]

SUMMARY

* *Symptoms can include self-destructive behaviors, splitting, and depression. See page 134.*

* *Promiscuity and drug/alcohol abuse are touted and overemphasized by some as the symptoms to look for in a borderline. Yet suicidal behavior, depression, and an inborn inability to control emotions appear as hallmark symptoms.*

* *Borderline personality disorder may be further complicated by other disorders occuring at the same time, such as post traumatic stress disorder (PTSD) or anorexia nervosa.*

* *Seeking professional treatment is of the utmost importance for individuals with BPD.*

* *Information on therapists in your area can be found through organizations like your local Mental Health Association, the American Psychiatric Association, or referrals from friends.*

Chapter 3

❨ INPATIENT HOSPITALIZATION

Longer Term Care

In this chapter, hospitalization in a treatment facility specifically devoted to psychiatric disorders will be discussed. Peggy, Emily, Isabelle, and Kimberly came to Highland Hospital via referrals by psychiatrists who worked with them either in outpatient or inpatient settings, yet recognized the need for longer term care. General medical hospitals that treat most major medical problems might have psychiatric units or wards, but they are not equipped or staffed to handle long-term (beyond a few weeks, usually) treatment. That is, most patients are hospitalized in such a unit for medication adjustments and crisis intervention, or they are there for intermediary stays before moving on to drug/alcohol rehabilitation, incarceration for legal offenses, or commitment to state hospitals or longer term care in hospitals specializing in the patient's suspected or definitive diagnosis.

It is significant to note that many hospitals are moving away from longer term care. A larger discussion of possible disadvantages of longer term care and the insurance trends that dictate the fiscal reality for many hospitals and patients are included in a later chapter. However, there are many advantages to longer term care. Partial hospitalization and shorter term care place a great deal of responsibility on the patient—in other words motivation to move toward wellness must be sparked quickly. The inpatient model of DBT used at Highland was adapted from Dr. Linehan's outpatient model. Initially, Dr. Linehan saw DBT skills training as an outpatient activity. However, safety must be the primary concern, and for high-risk parasuicidal patients, longer term care might be the safest solution initially. It takes time to motivate a depressed person, even more time for that person to realize they are motivated by something beyond the need to act on urges to self-harm.

> The prospect of long-term care can be daunting if not totally destabilizing to any psychiatric patient, including the hyper-sensitive borderline patient. For one thing, not even the smartest psychiatrist can tell a patient how long their stay will be. My doctor said she thought it would be a matter of two to three months. *Months?!*
>
> —MFT

Fear of the unknown with high-risk, suicidal patients is one of the primary reasons patients with BPD are placed in local hospital units for intermediary stays, and the patient normally is transferred directly from the local hospital. Some patients are allowed to be transported by family members, others, because of extreme suicidal tendencies or for medical reasons, are transported by ambulance. This all may seem frightening to contemplate until you have experienced the reality of such a system. It is set up to assure the safest possible transition for the patient, and yet you may feel as though you've suddenly slipped into a "twilight zone" where you are no longer in control of even your smallest needs.

I arrived at the hospital with my father, stepmother, and husband. The drive was a long one, and we were tired and nervous when we entered the building to which we had been referred. It was New Year's Day and was just growing dark. Hope and gathering foreboding mingle in that memory. It would be many months before I realized that the sun was always behind the moon in an eclipse. It would shine again, warm my face and brighten my world— a world in which I would choose to live. But, I didn't know that then and tears and a tight embrace came when it was time for my family to leave. I felt as though something was being wrenched out of me without anesthesia. I clung most tightly to my husband, whose white face and tears matched mine. He recalls having no idea what he was leaving me to face.

Would my days be spent with doctors, hour upon hour in an intensive treatment setting? That was my husband's notion, and he was horrified to learn later that I saw my psychiatrist thirty minutes, once a week, except for five minute discussions during daily rounds. I spent two hours a week with my therapist (psychologist). We weren't acquainted with the "team approach" yet. We would learn.

—MFT

Upon admission to Highland, the patient and any present family members receive an interview with the primary physician in charge of the patient's care. All luggage is searched and patients are asked to remove their shoes and empty their pockets. It feels a bit degrading, but it is meant to prevent harmful objects from entering the hospital environment.

Highland has several units: BPD, dual diagnosis programs (drug and/or alcohol dependency), short-term admissions/general psychiatry, Multiple Personality Disorder (MPD), and adolescent units. Each is set up with regulations specifically designed for the patient's benefit. Not all units are in the same building and those that are are separated by floors. Still, the patients find they mingle with many differently diagnosed patients during activities that take place off the unit.

I suppose the first question someone who has not been to a psychiatric institution might have is, "what does it look like"? I thought it looked a lot like a well-groomed college campus, with dormitories, a cafeteria, and office buildings blending in with the surrounding landscaping. In fact, Highland offers a pleasant appearance with a wooded area behind the buildings, some of which date back to the hospital's founding in 1904. Okay, okay, the showers leave a little to be desired. But, the water stayed warmer longer than I had experienced in the hospital ward in my hometown. The tile just looked a bit cracked and worn, and I missed a bathtub filled with fragrant bubbles. But, so, too, does many a college student.

—*MFT*

In other aspects, the floor of the BPD unit resembled those of my hometown hospital. The nurses' station was in the center of the unit, with patient rooms stretching down both sides of a long hallway. The doors could be closed, but not locked. There were single and double rooms. Most were doubles with twin beds, and many had a bath adjoining to the next room. Although spartan, furnishings were adequate, complete with dressers, separate closets and a writing desk and chair. Rather than a hospital room, my room looked like a college dorm before the dirty laundry, scattered notebooks, makeup, and backpack descended.

At one end of the hall, a pair of glass doors led to "the living room"—a couch- and chair-filled room with a TV, piano, aquarium, magazines, an exercise bicycle, and shelves filled with puzzles and other games that looked used if not abused over the years. The opposite end of the hall led to a tiny laundry room with a table and two chairs, an ice dispenser and soda vending machine, a sink, refrigerator and cabinets. Later, I learned that access to the laundry on the weekends was almost impossible and nightly snacks were delivered to the unit explaining the kitchenette.

> A footnote on the "laundry quandary": When I had been in the hospital a mere few days, I saw on someone's closet door her name on two separate sheets of paper. "God, am I losing it? Is she losing it? Will I one day have to put my name on pieces of paper to remind myself who I am each morning?" The next day I saw this woman working efficiently in the laundry room. She put her load of clothes in the dryer, then she stuck

one of the papers with her name to the machine in case it finished before her return. Lost underwear and socks were one of the continuing complaints on the unit, as was the fact that nobody ever let another patient know when their laundry was done before tossing their clothes out and taking over the machines. This woman wasn't losing it. She had things pretty well in hand, I'd say.

—*MFT*

The most daunting thing about the place was a glance at any window. They were gridded—not with the thick bars made famous in westerns—but with thin bars, assuring "this is *not* an exit." In fact, all patients leaving and returning to the unit signed in and out with the date and time included. Failure to do so could bring a loss of privileges. This is standard procedure at Cornell, Westchester Division, too. Such a procedure can lead to a claustrophobic feeling, even cries of "Am I really so crazy that I belong here?"

As one borderline poignantly phrased it, "I'm only seventeen. I should be going to my prom, but I'm stuck in a mental hospital." The reality of the matter is that she could not conduct herself safely at a prom or any other place outside of the controlled setting of the hospital. She was splitting and seeing the outside world as "good" and the inside world as "bad." She didn't yet realize that this inside world offered her the most promise of enjoying the outside world. Moreover, other patients often told her that she was lucky getting help at such an early age. She would have more years of wellness ahead of her than most of the patients (who ranged in age from late twenties to mid-forties). These are middle-of-the-road types of rationalizations that borderlines, young and older, have a tremendously difficult time accepting when it comes to themselves.

Emily phrases it best. "It's like we can be mirrors for each other but not for ourselves. I can look at Isabelle and get really upset that she's starving herself. She looks at the cuts on my arms and tells me that she cares about my safety and me as a person and that I need to throw away my dangerous behavior. We borderlines sure do care for others. Do we give it all away and not save anything of caring for ourselves?"

Isabelle's second return to Highland Hospital brought back bad memories and caused her to panic. Her admission did not proceed as smoothly as might have been hoped. After all, she had been to the facility before and knew what to expect. She was met courteously until her own behavior skyrocketed out of control. Even then, the staff continued to treat her with courtesy while putting in place recommended controls on her (ward restriction) until her primary physician could feel more optimistic about her ability to conduct herself appropriately around other patients in settings off the ward. Isabelle readjusted rather quickly, given these restrictions, and was able to set up an activity schedule the next day.

Typical Day

An example of a typical activity schedule is included to help give a sense of "a day in the life" of an inpatient. Getting into the swing of a routine can be difficult, especially at the beginning of an admission. This example is from Highland Hospital where Dr. William Barley gave DBT classes, which he continues at Charter-Asheville:

Sample Schedule for Personality Disorder Program

	Monday	Tuesday	Wednesday	Thursday	Friday	Saturday	Sunday
8:15-8:40	Rounds	Rounds	Rounds	Rounds	Rounds		
8:40-9:30	Rounds	Rounds	Rounds	Rounds	Rounds		
9:30-10:20	Anger Management	PD Group	Anger Management	Stress Group	Group Therapy	Rounds	Rounds
10:30-11:20	Long Track Homework	Women's Group	Self-Monitor Group	Long Track Homework			Core Skills Diary Cards
11:30-12:20	Referral Groups	Referral Groups	Referral Groups	Referral Groups	Referral Groups		
12:30-1:30	Lunch	Lunch	Lunch	Lunch	Lunch	Lunch	Lunch
1:30-2:20	Referral Groups	Referral Groups	Referral Groups	Referral Groups	Referral Groups	Community Leisure Activities	Community Leisure Activities
2:30-3:20	Short Track DBT	Milieu Meeting	Short Track DBT		Short Track DBT		
3:30-4:30	Group Therapy	Long Track DBT	Community Meeting	PD Program Meeting	Long Track DBT		
4:30-5:30							
5:30-6:30	Dinner	Dinner	Dinner	Dinner	Dinner	Dinner	Dinner
6:30-7:20	PDP Pt. Govt. Meeting	Short Track Homework	Worship Service				
7:30-8:30	Tools For Crisis Survival And Relaxation						

Irregularities occur in the schedule—for example the weekly appointments with the psychiatrist and therapist take precedence over an activity. So, too, do things such as dental appointments and physical exams by a general practitioner or consults with other medical specialists which result in necessary scheduling changes.

Doctor's Rounds

Perhaps one of the biggest shocks patients have at Highland is the concept of group rounds. Group therapy sessions were the first order of business at New York Hospital's Cornell Westchester Division and rounds were not conducted in a group setting. However, at Highland, rounds take place each morning at a specified time, and to miss them is unacceptable. The first consequence of missing rounds is having privileges revoked. However, if a patient continually misses mandatory activities and meetings it can be cause for discharge from the hospital. If a patient takes no interest in engaging in treatment, hospitalization cannot help. Such behavior can be viewed as an example of treatment interfering behavior. This receives high priority, second only to self-harm, in the hierarchy of treatment. While it might appear that this patient is treatment-resistant, DBT therapists see such behavior as part of the borderline disorder and attempt to work with the patient from that point of view. Unfortunately, few alternatives are left to those patients who simply will not work toward change. Change is the mainstay of DBT skills; maladaptive behavior is not invalidated, but it is targeted for change.

If a patient continues to not engage in any of the structure of their treatment after adequate private discussions with therapists and their psychiatrist, the patient might be asked to leave the hospital. Patients who are asked to leave are often invited to re-enter the program within a few weeks. They are contacted to see if they are ready to give the hospital program and DBT therapy another chance. If life outside the hospital is unbearable and life inside the hospital is unworthy of participation, the overall prognosis is grim. Patients sometimes remind one another of this reality when they are feeling unmotivated. Pep talks are frequent and helpful. The treatment team and the patient team often complement each other in significant ways.

During rounds, usually the primary physician asks what kind of progress you are noting, activities in which you are involved, and medications are discussed. If you are embarrassed about side effects or requesting special medication for, say, a yeast infection, you are out of luck. You have to become accustomed to discussing these things in front of a group. Depending upon the patients with whom you are housed, you may hear snickers, especially if there are male patients present (see Appendix C). The overwhelming majority of patients diagnosed with BPD are women, however. Soon, shyness passes and the individual personality of the milieu seeps through. The group rounds concept has its pros and cons. At many hospitals it is a matter of expediency. Since Highland uses the team approach, it hardly would seem feasible to arrange the schedules of the individual patient, primary physician, social worker, primary nurse, and psychiatric aides for each DBT unit resident on a daily basis.

Even aside from scheduling, though, the group approach has other, more subtle advantages to recommend it. For instance, if one patient is particularly reticent, and continually fails to cite examples of their own progress, members of the group might begin to say something like a mumbled, "she reached out to us last night, and asked if she could join our card game. We were glad to see her coming out of her shell." This information can be extremely beneficial to the doctor who can't seem to get through to some patients. Naturally, the primary responsibility for giving progress notes falls to the patient. But, the group dynamic can be of assistance in this way and others.

Emily, whose illness seemed to embolden her, never failed to speak up or even back to doctors, nurses, other patients, and/or the social worker. Her mind is quick as a whip and her temper is just one step behind. If Emily felt the doctor moved past her chart too quickly before she was able to formulate a question, she would say, "Hey, I wasn't finished." Sometimes she would get an apology, other times she would hear that rounds were running behind and she could leave a message for the doctor at the nurses' station. Her ability to stick up for herself greatly impressed and even influenced Isabelle, who tended to shrink from the slightest hint of confrontation. Had it not been for group rounds, Isabelle might not have seen how others can stick up for themselves.

Rounds are conducted early in the morning, and mark an important start to the day. Results of medical tests are reported, patients request sleeping medications or medicines for other purposes, new patients are introduced and usually only asked how they are orienting to the unit, and the doctor often announces who has appointment times scheduled that day. One day a week is "Team Request Day." This is when patients ask for a raise in their privilege level. They may request visitors, off-grounds passes, and the like. Results are reported during the next day's rounds. A similar system exists at New York Hospital's Cornell, Westchester Division.

Today, DBT has been implemented at group homes, institutions, individual therapy, outpatient (as it began with Linehan's model), and many more settings. In fact, Dr. Charles Swenson began the job of national and international training for professionals in DBT in all of these settings.

On weekends and holidays the doctor makes appointed rounds. At one time this was not required by insurance companies and was not practiced at Highland. Patients would sleep a little later or take advantage of the time for their passes, etc. Today, the doctors at the hospital are on-call for one another's rounds. This enables special medication requests to be made during these times, and is likely of benefit to those who would sleep the day away in depression if not required to attend.

Regular activity schedules do not take place on weekends, so patients must engage themselves in some form of constructive distraction. Sleeping all day is frowned upon and charted, whereas a lively game of Scrabble® or one patient's plan for a Kentucky Derby Party is viewed in a positive, therapeutic light.

A patient who loved horses, reserved the TV via a note on the chalkboard (the accepted way to reserve the TV), and invited all interested patients to join her for the pre-race hype. She was a reserved, practically withdrawn woman, whose sudden enthusiasm was contagious. Instead of a boring Saturday in May, it became a time of excitement and bonding among women on the unit. She single-handedly brought others out of their depression, if only for a day or an hour.

The Patient Team

As mentioned previously, the group dynamic is of exceptional importance in treatment. Emily wisely observed, "We're so much alike, so sensitive, that there always seemed to be conflicts of one sort or another on the unit. You never know what to say to avoid sending another patient over an emotional hill." Yet, learning to live together in a community setting, resolving smaller conflicts without professional intervention, makes it easier to integrate into life after hospitalization.

The BPD unit includes community meetings in which conflicts could be resolved and/or kudos (i.e., a week without anyone conducting self-harm—Hooray!) given. Dr. Peterson, the nurses, and PAs are present only as facilitators, sensitive to the possibility of too painful emotional arousal. A separate weekly patient meeting is held by the patients only, with small dues collected for future discharge parties and special purchases that are voted on and decided by majority. A unit president, vice president, treasurer/secretary are elected to run this meeting, and once a week the officers report to the nursing director any decisions or appropriate requests. Three to four VCR movies are rented per weekend; titles are voted on in the unit meeting and reported to staff for pickup on Friday. Naturally, conflicts arise and are settled. After all, attending college, pursuing careers, running a household, and raising children all involve conflict resolution skills and compromises. The hospital unit is a microcosm of life, albeit a highly controlled one.

Difficult Times

Poor patients who arrive on a chaos night! One arrived on the unit during a particularly difficult evening. It

seems that everyone was behaving inappropriately, or
"going off" (the Domino Effect, which is explained in
Chapter 4) in one fashion or another. They were yelling
and screaming, running or withdrawing, sometimes
behind furniture. The less structured evenings seemed
to give patients more time to ruminate on bad thoughts
or act on inappropriate urges.

This new patient came in and wondered, "what have I
gotten myself into?" But, after about half an hour, things
settled down, and Peggy and Isabelle went to greet her
and try to make her feel less alone by watching TV with
her in the lounge. "When Isabelle talked to me and told
me that she had tried at one time to cut off her stomach
because she felt overweight", this new patient suddenly
felt, "I'm in the right place, I do have something in
common with these women."

Some patients feel the same way. Even as outrageous
as the described behavior might sound to someone
outside the realm of BPD, to this person it was like
docking in a familiar harbor. At Highland, she knew
she could disclose her serious self-injury, and she could
work with doctors and a treatment team who understand
and would try to help rather than berate her. However,
DBT discourages the discussion of previous parasuicidal
behavior outside the therapeutic group or individual
settings.

Not long after the new patient's arrival, Peggy and Kim
prevented Isabelle from spending an evening in the "quiet
room" and from having her privileges reduced by stopping
an escape attempt. It was evening, that difficult time for
many patients, when structure is low and free time
mounts. Isabelle saw Kim limping down the hall (she
had a broken foot in a cast) and asked her in a serious

voice, "I'm going for it, wanna join me?" Kim thought it was a joke, because the thought of the two of them making it out the door (unlocked for a supervised five minute smoking break) was absurd. She answered, "Sure. Wait 'til I get my shoe." Then Isabelle headed for the door, full speed ahead. Peggy, who was in the front lobby, stopped her, but couldn't hold her down by herself. Kim's motherly instincts also came to the fore, and she helped. They held Isabelle and talked to her soothingly. Later they all were able to laugh at the extreme irrationality of the entire episode. Isabelle said, "You two would make great PAs!" They replied, "Hell, you're stronger than you look!"

Although this incident worked out safely, the hospital does not recommend that patients take each other's safety into their own hands. Peggy and Kim could have been injured by a violent Isabelle. Even Emily's observation of caring for others more than one's self, is viewed at times as a behavior that interferes with treatment.

This issue arises repeatedly on the unit. Sometimes a patient will know of another's plan to hurt themselves. It feels like tattling, but the staff expects such knowledge to be reported. The most effective way of doing this is to give the patient an opportunity to turn to the staff on their own. A realistic scenario is: "I'm going to stand here and watch you for five minutes. Then, if you haven't gone to the nurses' station with that broken glass, I will because I care about your safety." There is no such thing as confidentiality when it comes to parasuicide.

The quiet room consists of a mattress and a door with a small, wire-meshed glass observation window. When patients get out of control, they are escorted to this room and often sleep there, observed all night by staff. No paper or pens or any other paraphernalia is allowed in the room, as anything might become a weapon in such an agitated person's hand. Patients sometimes request to go into the quiet room. If they are frightened by the noises on the unit (including the verbal outbursts common in the evenings) or if they feel unsafe, they can request to sleep there supervised. Patients feeling on the edge of "going off" also have requested to use the quiet room, where they scream into the mattress, or find other means of settling themselves down, without causing a disruption on the unit.

If a patient sleeps in the quiet room overnight, the mattress is made up to keep the patient warm and comfortable; however if out of control behavior, such as banging the head against the wall continues, restraints may have to be used. These are leather buckles that immobilize the patient face down on the mattress with their hands and feet secured. One PA said, "If my job consisted merely of placing patients in restraints, it would not be worth it. But, thankfully, counseling patients on a one-to-one basis and participation in team treatment make up the majority of my job. I feel like I am listened to and able to listen. It's a good feeling."

Activity Therapy

Scheduled activities or "classes" are set up on an individual case basis between the patient and the unit's assigned activity therapist. Then the schedule should be approved by the patient's primary physician, and may be a matter of discussion during team meetings.

The team approach used at Highland, involves primary nurses, psychiatrists, psychologists, psychiatric assistants, activity therapists, nutritionists, and social workers who, together, evaluate a patient's progress. This meeting is closed to patients and gives these professionals a forum for honest feedback and observations regarding each patient's individual involvement and progress in hospital activities and therapeutic settings.

A patient's activity schedule can be a topic of team meetings since one member's knowledge of something can influence decisions regarding important scheduled events. For example, Peggy was suffering one of the most severe cases of depression her primary physician and her therapist had witnessed. They had clear examples from Peggy that showed inappropriate, non-supportive behavior on the part of her husband. Therefore, although her social worker suggested a visit from her husband and children to the team, a more modest approach was recommended during Peggy's early weeks at the hospital. Telephone calls with a speaker phone were made to Peggy's husband (and sometimes children) with her social worker present. The social worker operated as a mediator and consultant to Peggy when the dialogue deteriorated or things threatened to go out of control.

Team members try to be consultants to other members rather than interveners during team deliberations. Team members also consult with patients about how to deal with other team members.

For patients with eating disorders, the nutritionist's Body Image class was mandatory. Isabelle was placed in this class against her will and in conflict with her desire to take Physical Fitness in its place. The team further recommended that she be restricted only to more sedentary activities during her early weeks of hospitalization.

Patients who appeared to suffer from depression related to overwhelming schedule demands, or conversely, too little to do at home were referred to Leisure Education class. This class offers testing to determine interests from careers to hobbies and assists in structuring a balanced active/leisurely week for participants.

Some patients are given more freedom in developing schedules and can choose, based on interest and/or experience, from a variety of classes including Horticulture, Photography, Spirituality, Aerobics, and Relaxation, just to name a few. Some patients without Peggy's particular situation also experienced more flexibility in planning special events such as family visits. In fact, Highland strongly advocates family interaction with patients through visits, if geographically feasible, or regular telephone calls and letter writing.

Naturally, individual and group therapy sessions, meal and medication times, doctors' rounds, and DBT skills training groups become a mandatory part of a borderline patient's schedule. Younger patients who still attend secondary school sometimes have to trade doctor's appointments with other patients to fit them all in, but they are never excused (except due to physician-recognized physical illness) from the mandatory activities. Highland does have a school on the premises, and this makes it a bit easier. Patients do have a busy day, with only a few breaks between classes. However, patients adapt to this and know there will be free time in the evenings. This evening time becomes a haven for some and an interminable period for others. Watching the news on television, initiating a Scrabble® game with others, riding an exercise bicycle, writing, journaling, reading, completing DBT class assignments, or listening to music keeps most patients sufficiently distracted until "med or bed" time or the evening one-to-one session with their assigned psychiatric aide.

Journaling is something that most therapists ask their patients to undertake. It involves writing about your day paying particular attention to times when your emotions seemed strongest—either good or bad. Recording memories from dreams in the journal is helpful to the therapist also. Noting how your one-to-ones went, what you processed with your assigned PA, and basically any significant events in the day or evening that can help point toward what triggered your emotions, and what your reactions to them were can become a powerful tool for patient and therapist.

One-to-Ones

Psychiatric aides provide an invaluable service to patients in hospital settings, whether on short-term wards or in longer care facilities. Highland recognized this importance when they established a system for patients to check-in with a staff member assigned to them twice daily. The schedule for check-in goes up in the morning, normally right after doctors' rounds. It is significant that it is the patient's responsibility to initiate contact with their aide and agree to a scheduled time to meet. This is the case at New York Hospital's Cornell, Westchester Division, as well. The daily check-ins sometimes are abbreviated due to the rigorously scheduled day for patients and staff meetings, as well. However, it is extremely important for this staff member to hear from the patient's own lips whether feelings of loneliness, suicide, aggressive/agitated are being experienced. Suicidal feelings obviously become a major concern to the aide, and further precautions may be taken.

For instance, if a patient reveals a plan and admits to having the means to carry out the plan, usually they are placed on constant observation. If time permits during an evening check-in, the aide normally will try to process these feelings with the patient, giving the patient a way to vent and perhaps lessen the feelings through having revealed them. Also, the discussion between patient and PA sometimes helps reveal a stressor or event that could have brought such feelings to the surface. Peggy often felt suicidal before and after scheduled phone conversations with her husband. Emily, though by nature more secretive about her urges to harm herself, learned that they were preceded by a feeling of being in danger or from a nightmare. All of these data are charted and become significant pieces in the puzzle the team so diligently works on—with the goal of a life worth living.

Privilege Levels

We have discussed, briefly, my own and Isabelle's ward restriction and a suicidal patient's constant observation. Every psychiatric hospital that I know about uses some system of privileges/liberties/levels for their patients. It is easy to make a casual observation that this is a way to control and motivate patients. True. But, dialectically speaking, there is another important role that privilege levels occupy in the hospital setting. Safety of the patients is the number one priority. In fact, some patients request to be placed on a lower privilege level for their own safety. Just as a patient might recognize their own state of agitation and ask to use the quiet room, this is an example of the patient using problem-solving skills to avoid self-harm.

Given too many freedoms, off-grounds privileges for example, a highly suicidal patient might take the opportunity to buy (or shoplift) harmful items. At Highland, all bags are checked upon return from such outings. Even this isn't a fool-proof system though, as patients might sign themselves back in and toss contraband into their rooms before proceeding to the nurses' station for the search. Another, more frightening, scenario is that the one who searches may not recognize the danger of some item(s).

Isabelle diligently worked her way up the privilege system at Highland during her first stay. She appeared to be a model patient, taking notes during DBT class and asking questions. Yet, team members sensed she was bottling something up. She just kept saying she was "fine" during one-to-ones, citing a recent letter from a friend or another special reason for feeling okay. After one of her shopping excursions (taken with other patients—the next to highest privilege level available), Isabelle attempted to extinguish her life by using the plastic bag in which her purchased items had come. No record of attempted asphyxiation was on her chart, so there was no perceived need for alarm during check-in. She nearly was successful, but her timing was not perfect. Fifteen minute checks on all patients are made at Highland. The psychiatric aide who opened Isabelle's door saw the entire scene in time to prevent unconsciousness.

Yes, Isabelle lost privilege levels that night. She very nearly lost her life, the failure of which at first seemed only to anger her. She was haughty when questioned about the seriousness of her behavior. "I know I could have died quickly, that's why I did it." The team had only begun to scratch the surface of Isabelle's sexual abuse. Once more pieces of her case were put together painstakingly by Isabelle as well as therapists, the patient moved higher up the privilege system, and gladly turned over any plastic bags after signing in. Life, Isabelle was learning, is far too precious to extinguish.

Just as an example of what to expect in terms of privileges in a facility such as Highland, the privilege levels usually correlate to something like constant observation, fifteen minute self-check, and ward restriction. Then, higher privileges are available in four levels. Many patients begin on ward restriction. That gives the patient freedom to interact with other patients while on the ward and to write, read, journal, etc. However, they must eat from a meal tray rather than joining the others in the dining hall, and are restricted from all but the mandatory scheduled activities. This is not the lowest level on the hierarchy, but it is where many patients begin if the team does not feel they have enough data to move them to the next higher level. The Level 1 privilege allows patients to maintain their entire schedule, but they must be escorted to and from all off-ward activities, including doctor appointments. Further, visits by family and friends are restricted to the hospital grounds.

Patients deemed a danger to themselves or others are placed on constant observation. They are ward-restricted and must have a staff member within arm's reach of them at all times. Yes, that includes bathroom activities as degrading as it may sound. However, the bathroom is a dangerous place for the suicidal—and desperation often is the mother of invention. One patient managed to slit her wrists with a toothpaste tube! Fifteen minute self-checks allow the ward-restricted patient to voluntarily initial a time-chart at the nurses' station at the appropriate time. Patients also must mark their mood at the time of check-in, i.e., agitated, suicidal, calm, as appropriate.

Level 2 gives patients freedom to maintain their schedules while going to doctor's appointments unescorted. When family members and/or friends visit, off-ground privileges are extended to the patient. Level 3 enables patients to go to all scheduled activities unescorted. It also offers the opportunity to request off-grounds privileges with at least one other patient who has Level 3 or higher privileges. This extends opportunities for off-grounds outings, as family and friends are not always, even generally, geographically available for regular visits. These requests for outings go to the team meeting once a week, and are approved based on the appropriateness of the request and the participants' recent behavior.

Such outings can be fun, even to the depressed. Often patients will dress up for a trip to the movies or a restaurant with other patients, and while out, experience a sense of reintegrating into society. The outing also gives them a chance to make important purchases, such as personal hygiene items or scented lotion or soap that can make a person with very little of life's happiness feel better.

Level 4 is the highest privilege level offered at Highland. It gives the patient a chance to request off-grounds privileges alone for a set period of time. This level is granted most often near the end of a patient's stay and for the purpose of assisting their reintegration process. Some patients report a high level of anxiety about calling a taxi on their own. Others express the sheer joy of freedom in randomly browsing bookstores and antique shops without having to phone in to anyone until their pass expires.

Sometimes, an upbeat week whether from successful passes, absence of self-harmful behavior or whatever might bring out the cleverness of the patients. Dr. Peterson has a mustache and wears glasses which gives him a small resemblance to one of the Marx brothers (who shall remain nameless). While he was away for a holiday, the patients felt some abandonment although their rounds were covered by qualified doctors and their feelings were aired in different meetings. To greet Dr. Peterson's return, each patient wore a black and white outfit along with the nose/mustache glasses sold in gag gift stores. It went over well, especially since he didn't notice anything at first. He was busy with charts and pulled Kim's up first. He looked up, saw her disguise and then laughed, or rather bellowed, for some time. "You have been so depressed that this just makes my day!" he said. Then he looked around and saw that all of his patients were involved and he laughed even harder. It feels good to laugh in a mental hospital. It feels good to make others laugh in that setting, as well.

Sometimes though, laughter isn't appropriate. Two patients, dubbed Positron and Negatron by themselves, complete opposites of one another, somehow formed a thorny friendship. Positron was by nature optimistic and held onto hope for her future and that of her fellow patients. Negatron had been on many different antidepressants and even when she felt "okay" she always bemoaned the fact that, "This won't last. It never does." Together, they made a unique team. Positron was like a nerve-splitting Pollyanna to Negatron, who would gripe at her slightest suggestion that something better might be around the corner. But, each time Negatron disputed what her friend said, the irritating thing would come back with yet another argument. What did Positron get out of all of this? It made her work harder and harder to see something positive. As for Negatron, it made it harder and harder to see only the negative.

Once, Negatron shared the words of a song that were given to her by another patient in another hospital (Negatron had had her share of life's down side, as have most probably all borderline patients). The page the song was written on was wrinkled and yellow with age. Positron offered to type a new copy for her friend. They received permission to use the unit typewriter, and Positron tapped out several copies, one for herself. It made more than a big difference in the lives of two women—it made them both feel better one day in a psychiatric hospital; they felt useful and alive.

> My therapy took a big step backward when my 40-year-old brother died unexpectedly of heart failure. The youngest of four children, I had looked to this brother as almost a third parent, and he filled in beautifully. He made me feel special and like I could do anything I set my mind to do. It was the opposite when significant people in my life made the chauvinistic statement: "You're married; do you really need a career?" Just days before his death, my brother sent me a card that later would figure prominently in my healing process. In it, he wrote, "Be gentle with yourself—you're only human, you know, and we are a species that abounds in frailties and imperfections. Nonetheless we do manage to accomplish some grand and wondrous things, and among these is the simple joy of living through a single day with hope and appreciation for the good in ourselves and the blessings of the love and

friendship which we receive from others. You are rich in all of these."

—*MFT*

Much later, Isabelle, too, would begin to assimilate that the loss of trust and the loss of loved ones need not be the loss of all that is good and meaningful in a person. The power of good memories filled her eyes with tears, but her heart with joy, and she knew that her mother and once-alcoholic father would always be a part of her. They would not just be a part of her life, but an integral part of who she is and who she would be. It was up to Isabelle to discern what aspects of them she would carry forward in herself through oral history, traditions, and all the means in which one conveys something inside to the outside world.

Dr. Sue Chance appears to share some thoughts with the more assimilated Isabelle. In her book, *Stronger Than Death,* she elegantly states, "And, when we come to…that first and final place, I think we will finally perceive the fact that, during all our travel, the electrons of those we have loved were orbiting gently through our hearts."

Profound thoughts and words, tears, unexpected friendships, and the ability to joke and keep a sense of humor—that was the Brownian Movement at Highland Hall when Positron, Negatron, Isabelle, Peggy, Emily, Kimberly, and others were members of the same milieu. It also was a healthy demonstration of the reality of emotions and relationships in life outside of a hospital setting.

Emotions are a mixture, which, like many different colors help to paint a complete picture. Life is not one thing, nor is it comprised of a single feeling or emotion. It need

not be, and is richer, more textured for the many com-
ponents that make up its seasons.

> *Included next is a handout from Dr.
> Linehan's model: Myths about Emo-
> tions, that DBT students complete. It
> helps dispel that thought that there is
> only one correct response to any given
> situation. The broad range of responses
> from students in a DBT session helps
> bring to light the true texture of emo-
> tions and responses.*

Myths about Emotions

1. There is a right way to feel in every situation.
CHALLENGE: _____
2. Letting others know that I am feeling bad is weakness.
CHALLENGE: _____
3. Negative feelings are bad and destructive.
CHALLENGE: _____
4. Being emotional means being out of control.
CHALLENGE: _____
5. Emotions can just happen for no reason.
CHALLENGE: _____
6. Some emotions are really stupid.
CHALLENGE: _____
7. All painful emotions are a result of a bad attitude.
CHALLENGE: _____
8. If others don't approve of my feelings, I obviously shouldn't feel the way I do.
CHALLENGE: _____
9. Other people are the best judge of how I am feeling.
CHALLENGE: _____
10. Painful emotions are not really important and should be ignored.
CHALLENGE: _____
11.
CHALLENGE: _____
12.
CHALLENGE: _____
13.
CHALLENGE: _____
14.
CHALLENGE: _____
15.
CHALLENGE: _____

SUMMARY

❧ *Psychiatric units in general medical hospitals are sometimes used during times of crisis or medication adjustments.*

❧ *A highly suicidal person may need longer term care in a specialized hospital for their own safety.*

❧ *It takes time to motivate a highly suicidal and depressed individual. Sometimes longer term care provides more opportunity for treatment to be successful.*

❧ *Scheduled activities in an inpatient setting may include group therapy, individual therapy, patient community meetings, and recreational therapeutic classes.*

❧ *DBT in an inpatient setting can include skills training classes and homework assignments.*

☾ Drawbacks to Longer Term Care

I t is true that while psychiatric hospitals with good
reputations and track records are not the horrors
depicted in movies such as *One Flew Over the Cuckoo's
Nest* and *Snake Pit,* there are documented drawbacks to
longer term care.

The Domino Effect

One commonly noted example of drawbacks is known
as the "Domino Effect." In essence this is the opposite of
our Kentucky Derby Queen's contagious enthusiasm. It
can take only one patient to bring an entire unit
down. Suicide attempts, so regularly engaged in by Kim
and some other borderlines on the unit, trigger a host
of emotions in the rest of the milieu. Others may mirror
her behavior, having been so unsettled by her attempt
as to be destabilized. This happens with self-inflicted
injuries such as cutting, which is literally cutting a part
of the body, usually the wrist or arm with a sharp object,
but sometimes the stomach and other parts. Cutting is

a common maladjusted behavior among borderlines. Once a patient chooses this form of behavior, several similar cases often are noted within a short period of time—even in the same week. A serious state of despondency seen in one patient can set the mood for the unit as well. While this might not appear to be as serious in some ways as actual "tissue damage" (the clinical name for most self-harmful events), if a patient becomes sarcastic and uncooperative during rounds and other unit meetings, agitation can spread like wildfire. In the hospital this type of phenomena is termed by the patients as "going off." "When I heard so and so shrieking all night and then her suite mate going off, I just lost control and went screaming down the hall," is a familiar line of conversation during rounds after such episodes. Witnessing escape attempts and seeing a patient "escorted" to the quiet room, finding your roommate huddled and despondent behind the nightstand, or even getting a snappish response from an overworked nurse or PA can tip the borderline over the edge.

Nights are usually the worst times. Phone calls to or from home have a fifteen minute limitation to allow as many people as possible to use the line. Most often many of these calls end with the patient in tears. It's nice to hear a voice from the outside world, one that loves you. It's difficult to hang up, lose that support, and once again remember the walls that enclose you, the doors that lock you in and away from your "real" life. Peggy, Kim, and Emily had a particularly hard time saying goodbye to their children. Sometimes, other patients' offers of comfort or distraction are welcomed at these times; sometimes though, a patient needs to cry, alone.

Institutionalization

Dr. Eric Peterson has noted for quite some time that a patient nearing discharge often experiences a regression even to the point of self-harm. During group rounds he learned from several of them that they did feel heightened agitation at the prospect of leaving a place they had found safe. They went as far as to admit that thoughts of harming themselves (with all three R's in mind) came to them because they knew it would likely mean postponing the discharge. Safety is an important factor, but so is the daily regimen to which the patients have become accustomed. This is especially true for those whose stays extend to six months or more. After all, their medication has been apportioned to them at an allotted time in prescribed amounts. Their schedules have been fixed, with free time available mostly at night when the unit doors are locked.

Once they leave the safety of the hospital, they might be faced, like Kimberly, with the needs of several children and easy access to her two most frequently used weapons—large doses of medicine and razor blades, or they might be faced, like Peggy, with a husband who simply thinks her problems are "all in her head" and she could make herself behave properly if she would use some spine. These patients do confront a frightening world.

I was prone to running. It was my way of attempting to escape. I ran if I had a disagreement with my husband at home; I ran while jogging; I ran in shopping centers. When I felt trapped by words, thoughts, or physical structures,

sometimes I ran intentionally in front of
cars. When I left the hospital, there would be no
strong PAs trained to stop me.

—MFT

The everyday world was frightening enough to drive
these women into the need for hospitalization. How
would they survive if they were released? The world
certainly had not changed during their hospitalization. The
answer is that through an effective combination of psychotherapy and Dialectical Behavior Therapy the women,
hopefully, had learned to change their responses to what
frightened and held them back.

Insurance Limitations

Yet another drawback of longer term care is that fewer
and fewer insurance policies are covering months of
inpatient care for mental and nervous disorders. For
patients this fact may mean they have to leave the hospital before they actually are ready and before they are
equipped with the skills they need to handle their world.

Although some patients absorbed the DBT lessons like
a thirsty sponge, their insurance did not allow for a long-
term inpatient stay. And, their violent reactions to any
feeling of despondency or rejection, especially on the part
of their outpatient therapist, drove them repeatedly to
frightening, life-threatening behaviors as an outpatient.

For clinicians at Highland Hospital and elsewhere,
fewer long-term stays create the prospect of developing a
speed course in DBT that can stick, while also developing more efficient outpatient treatment. Perhaps we're
moving toward a more sophisticated outpatient and/or
partial hospitalization system which, hopefully, insurance

companies will finally begin to recognize and cover. This is a much less expensive approach, and could help solve reintegration difficulties that so many inpatients experience. It all remains to be seen. (See Appendix B.)

The Old Taboos

Lack of education in the general community about mental and nervous disorders and their treatment means the old taboo of insanity hangs like a dense fog over treatment facilities and their patients. This makes reintegration into life after hospitalization difficult for patients. It doesn't matter whether the perceived taboo is based on emotion or reality; the difficulty remains. Emily returned to her job and found supportive co-workers, but a boss who placed her in an unchallenging position. Without discussion, he assumed she needed "less responsibility" and he was within his legal rights to reassign her. Emily took on this label of a person with reduced capabilities and internalized the notion that she was no longer able to perform her job adequately. Eventually, she ended up on disability—another label that made her feel just that—"dis-abled."

While disability is a godsend for many former patients who do not have sufficient financial resources, the public needs to be made aware that such a resource is an enabler rather than a tag of inability. How far have we come from the impressions made by Hollywood? Unfortunately, not far enough. Within the mental health community the analogy frequently is made that a person who returns to work or school after a serious bout with diabetes is greeted far differently than the "mental patient" who returns. Mental illness is a chemical imbalance requiring specialized medications and/or lifestyle changes—no different from diabetes. That truth is powerful.

SUMMARY

✎ *In a hospital setting, one patient's despondency or suicide attempt can negatively affect all the other patients in the unit.*

✎ *As a patient improves during longer term care and begins feeling safe in the structured hospital setting, release back into the "real world" can seem daunting.*

✎ *Fewer insurance plans are covering months of hospitalization.*

✎ *The stigma of mental illness continues among an underinformed public and can make return to the workforce after long-term care difficult.*

Smothered

Smothered.
    All I feel is smothered...
By my feelings of
    loneliness, hopelessness, sadness and
    utterly deep depression.

I can't see any light right now—
    All there is is darkness and
    the pressure—oh the pressure
    to participate...

To participate in anything
    is more than I can bear.

When will this heaviness lift?
    And, if it lifts—how long
    'til it lowers its boom again?

I'm so tired of waiting—hoping for a
    Brighter tomorrow—
I'm tired,
    So very tired.

"Rachel"
April, 19, 1993

Chapter 5

☾ DIALECTICAL BEHAVIOR THERAPY (DBT)

Development and Purpose

DBT was developed by Marsha Linehan, Ph.D., a clinical psychologist at the University of Washington in Seattle. She found that the usual behavioral and cognitive therapy methods and concepts were not effective with her parasuicidal patients. So, she developed Dialectical Behavior Therapy, a therapy that helps emotionally desperate, self-destructive people to use behavioral and cognitive methods and ideas even when they feel terrible and want to hurt themselves or die. DBT is a non-blaming, compassionate therapeutic approach which is based solidly on research data about what BPD is and how to treat it effectively. In her book *Skills Training Manual for Treating Borderline Personality Disorder,* Linehan provides the handouts for each series or "module" of skills of Dialectical Behavior Therapy.

Her book, *Cognitive-Behavioral Treatment of Borderline Personality Disorder,* is written on an academic level for clinicians. The skills manual that accompanies it, contains the objectives of each skills module, and the handouts that accompany them. This makes it more accessible and pertinent to patients and their families and others not trained in DBT. Perhaps more importantly, this skills manual includes accessible explanations of Linehan's theory of the borderline personality and the rationale and method of DBT. It is available through bookstores nationwide. Therefore, here I only attempt to highlight aspects of the therapy. (These highlights are based on Linehan's skills manual and different therapists might order the modules differently or otherwise change their content to fit the patient group he/she leads).

Testimonials

Rachel's advice is "hold on to the hope, the miracle might just be around the next corner. I also recommend Viktor Frankl's book *Man's Search for Meaning*. Frankl was in a Nazi concentration camp and never lost hope. How inspiring this has been to me. Don't give up."

Isabelle says she is sure DBT saved her life. "Not just one time, but several times my skills have prevented me from falling back on maladaptive behaviors—so I can tell myself— 'you've done it before, you can do it again.' I learned *never* to give up whatever spark of hope was there, because I believe the best of life is yet to come. I'm grateful and lucky and skilled to be here to experience it."

Isabelle transitioned from her mid twenties into her early-thirties as a borderline inpatient. She volunteers her time with abused children and hopes to raise children of her own someday.

P., who received treatment at Cornell's Westchester Division, admits "I didn't want any part of this thing called DBT. I thought it was like brainwashing. I refused to go to the lecture and homework sessions. But, I was interested in getting better, so I got hold of Linehan's book and began my own slow study through it. It began to make sense. I'll be 50 years old this year. I've been tormented by my illness for so long that suddenly I just realized if I'm going to make it this is the means. "I especially took hold of the relationship effectiveness skills" (referred to later in this chapter). In fact, P. now teaches the DEAR MAN skills (explained later in this chapter) to families of patients. She explains how the skills helped her obtain what she wanted in certain cases. P. relates to others in DBT terms and has improved tremendously from all reports since she threw away the fear of "brainwashing" and took on the "wise mind" spirit of DBT.

Rachel emphasizes a different aspect of DBT, that of taking care of yourself before you help others. "DBT has helped me since my long-term hospitalization, which began in 1993. Now I feel I have a chance to lead a productive life. Before, I was in and out of different hospitals since 1985. "Because I had trouble concentrating in general, DBT was hard for me to make sense of at first. But, if it helps just a little bit, keep going, there's hope, never stop going—it will make a difference."

Rachel says, "Using the crisis intervention skills helps me, and now I can concentrate. I'm reading again for the first time in over a decade, that's how much this therapy has helped me. When I do have a hard time, I bounce back faster—so no more long hospitalizations."

Rachel was 35 years old at the writing of this book and says she is ready to find what life has to offer and what she has to offer in return. She doesn't feel intimidated by the search, only happy that she has reached this point in her recovery. She might succeed very well in a permanent job or career.

Hierarchy of Treatment

The hierarchy of treatment is so important that a pyramid sketch of it was placed in the lounge above the television as a constant reminder to patients and professionals alike.

This is the prioritized list that DBT addresses:

1. *Safety first*
2. *Treatment-interfering behavior*
3. *Lifestyle (enjoyment) interfering behavior (or, behavior that interferes with the quality of life)*
4. *Skilled behavior*

The skills learned through DBT are arranged to address these problems in this order. Kim's frequent "cheeking" or stocking up on medications with overdosing in mind (by not swallowing them when they were administered) was taken to be the first and foremost behavior to curb.

The four goals in this list are considered first-stage targets in DBT. It could take one to two years for the patient to achieve stability, after which the therapy could move on to post traumatic stress disorder or other life events which contribute to the patient's distress. For example, the tragic loss of Kim's father was addressed, not on a daily basis on the unit, but in her later weekly therapy sessions. Why? Her first behavior, the "cheeking", could end her life before the link between her loss and depression could be rooted out and, hopefully, reconciled. Thus, the safety behavior is a priority.

All this information might come at you
fast and hard. Perhaps, at this point,
you could use a letter from a friend.

Dear Fellow Patient,

I know you probably are scared and feeling abandoned and lost in the maze of a hospital or structured outpatient setting. There are so many rules and regulations. You are expected to follow a strict schedule of activities, including a class on Dialectical Behavior Therapy (DBT). You've never heard of this therapy. And, at the moment, you can't even concentrate on a book, magazine, or TV. Even those require too much thought.

I assure you—you are not alone. Your fellow patients can become your on the spot acquaintances, maybe even friends. Some are more advanced into DBT because they have been part of it longer. Others are just starting out, like you, and still others are not at a point where the therapy makes any sense. Truly, you are not alone.

DBT was developed to first attend to your safety and then to enhance your life by teaching you skills that can and eventually do ease your pain. Right now, all you want is to ease the pain, to stop your interminable suffering. You, just as I do, have extremely self-destructive thoughts and perhaps means to carry them out. You think that will end the pain. It doesn't. The only difference between us right now is that I finally realized that the skills of DBT do work, and my suffering has eased. I can throw out my old bag of hurtful tricks and fill it with my new skills. They have become second nature. I reach for my new tricks first. You might be clinging to self-destructive thoughts and sometimes actions. You want to stop the pain and you are getting along the best way you know how. But, you've learned that these hurtful behaviors don't stop the inner suffering for long. You might be willing to try something new. Keep that open mind.

Don't worry about the difficulty of following along in DBT class with all these "modules" addressing different aspects of your life and your pain. The modules are repeated, and homework or, rather, "room-work" can be tutored if you ask a staff member to help you. Also, you can ask for help from your fellow patients. Sometimes this results in an informal study session where laughter and learning go hand in hand.

Don't let this therapy daunt you, or, worse, cause you to drop out of the program. That's a big, life-threatening mistake. Your concentration will improve. The repetition will one day begin to sink in. And, when intense pain overwhelms you, try one of your skills. Relax in a warm bubble bath, listen to a relaxation tape or soothing music, play a card game with your fellow patients. Talk to your staff member to see if they have more ideas for your particular feelings. You *can* do it. I am with you all the way.

— MFT

Following, I attempt to address the differences between Short and Long Track DBT classes. Further I introduce the modules of Dialectical Behavior Therapy. Some acronyms are used and emphasized as a means of helping students remember the important tenets of the material. At Highland, Dr. Barley held two hour-long classes a week called "Long Track DBT." This class went into more detail of each module and patients moved into the class once they completed the short-track program. "Short Track DBT" was an abbreviated version of Dr. Barley's long-track class. It attempted to introduce students to DBT and the theory of borderline personality disorder through each module as quickly as possible. This abbreviated class existed for two important reasons. Some patients might be discharged before they had an opportunity to go through all the modules of Long Track DBT, and, therefore, would lack essential knowledge of skills in certain areas. The second rationale behind Short Track DBT class, was to bring new patients up to speed with the other patients assigned to the Long Track class as rapidly as possible.

The lexicon of DBT is different from our everyday vocabulary. In fact it is so different that on her first day in Short Track class, Emily grumbled: "I feel like I've been dropped down into the middle of a damn calculus class!"

Yes, the terms used and skills required are demanding, but they are logical and life-saving. Rachel, who now attends a partial hospitalization program called day hospital at Cornell's Westchester Division strongly advises: "Don't give up. It takes time to become comfortable with the terms and concepts presented in DBT. But, one day things fall into place and make sense. And, I can honestly say that they've made a life saving difference for me."

Given enough practice, a patient learns to correct their golf grip almost before they reach for the club, to extend Dr. Peterson's analogy. At Highland, mandatory homework sessions are built into each patient's schedule, one for each Long Track session and one for each Short Track schedule. These homework sessions were presided over by a staff member, one whom the nurses and PAs disclosed to the patients helped them learn more about the therapy and skills and helped them in their counseling and other roles on the unit.

It is important to emphasize that skills training classes should be adjunctive to individual DBT therapy. That is, individual therapists must help patients apply their skills learned in class. It takes a lot of assimilation for a patient to reach for the skills in an intense emotional situation. Although more mental health professionals are learning DBT, sometimes patients must share their knowledge, handouts, etc. with an open-minded therapist who will learn along with and supplement the patient's attempt to integrate these skills.

That was the case for P. who says "now after 11 months of hospitalization at Cornell, I educate my therapist in my hometown. We work together on the skills. I wouldn't have made it through the last year without them, and I'm glad to share what I can."

SKILL MODULES

Core Skills

Turtles for One and All! Dr. William Barley teaches the DBT classes at Highland. He has been dubbed "Turtle Man" with good reason. He uses the "brainchild" (turtling) of Donald Meichenbaum, Ph.D., a Canadian psychologist who completed a significant amount of research on cognitive behavior therapy. Dr. Barley's first handout is a sketch of a cartoon turtle. The image is a reminder to pull your head in, take stock, and don't leap before you look for an impulsive behavior can be a dangerous behavior.

Dr. Barley encourages class participants to find their own "turtles." These are things that remind them of that very concept, yet don't have to resemble an actual turtle at all. For some it is a picture of their husband, a reminder that there is a reason to live. For Emily, it is her Raggedy Ann doll, that makes her feel safe and connects her to her children indirectly. For others, it may need to be an image of a turtle of some sort. The BPD unit at Highland is filled to overflowing with turtle posters, necklaces, T-shirts, puzzles, and a special turtle hat given to Dr. Barley as a Christmas gift. Gosh, it looked silly on him! But, it made people—deeply depressed people—laugh, or at least smile, when he'd don that hat and begin to talk about serious behavioral change mechanisms.

The Wise Mind

The concept of the "wise mind" is also presented up front in DBT. It is visualized as the synthesis or balance of the intellectual mind and the emotional mind. Here, black and white meet, and must be held in the wise mind simultaneously. It is in this realm that DBT functions. Note the diagram of Linehan's:

Taking Hold of Your Mind:

States of Mind

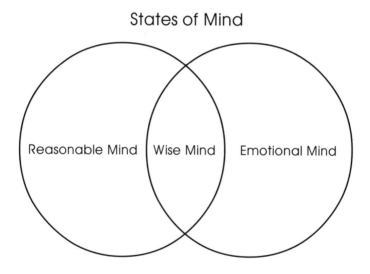

Reasonable Mind | Wise Mind | Emotional Mind

Mindfulness

Mindfulness is being completely aware yet nonjudgmental about what is happening to you. An example of mindfulness is this internal dialogue: "I am awake. I see a grey sky. I am cold. I hear the shower running and someone walking down the hall. I am pulling another cover over me. I feel warmer. I am not tired. I am sitting up and reading a magazine. I am not concentrating on the words in the magazine. I am concentrating on the pictures." This is stilted talk, yet it prevents such connections as "I see a grey sky, damn it's going to rain and be cold all day. I'd rather lie in bed than face this day." It also keeps a person in the present, not allowing them to wallow in past mistakes, painful memories, or fear of the future. It keeps them in a safe place. The key is remaining nonjudgmental. As soon as "I hear someone screaming," deteriorates into "They always scream and it makes me feel so angry I could go out there and give them a piece of my mind," it's time to change to another core skill that works for you or to return to mindfulness as often as necessary.

Mindfulness is taught first because it strengthens concentration and thinking skills, strengthens a sense of self, and increases access to the wise mind and tolerance. Mindfulness teaches nonjudgmental, mindful observation, description of inner and outer events, and effective participation in difficult situations and states of distress. The ability to be aware of an emotion and remain nonjudgmental is very empowering. For example, "I feel sadness. It is making my heart beat faster. I am aware of tears." How different this is from, "I'm in so much pain, I've got to end it any way I can!" Accepting sadness as an emotion and not judging it "good" or "bad" can help a person tolerate very difficult times. Observation skills are taught along with mindfulness. The emphasis on a nonjudgmental attitude remains important. Perhaps an upsetting scene comes on television in the hospital unit. No one else seems to be affected but it is getting to you. Distancing yourself from the situation, observing but not participating might be needed to get you through to the next commercial. These skills, mindfulness and observation, remain important underpinnings for all the DBT modules that follow.

Emotion Regulation Skills

Emotion regulation begins with information about emotion and the functions of one's feelings. Balancing extreme and invalidating beliefs about emotions increases understanding overall. This is the next module Linehan approaches in her training sessions with borderline individuals. The mindfulness and observation skills already covered can help borderlines in this module. Sometimes a person suffering from borderline personality disorder can't even name what emotion is creating so much distress.

The beginning exercises have much to do with relaxation techniques. Learning to breathe properly in order to calm oneself down can have a tremendous impact in an emotionally charged situation. One technique, called belly breathing requires some concentrating on the diaphragm while breathing, causing the belly rather than the chest to move in and out.

To show how effective this technique can be, look at the example of an anorexic patient at Highland who returned from an evening worship service in an extremely distressed state. The patient often attended these services, but this time she saw a woman who had been discharged from the hospital a year before. The other patient was "thin as a skeleton and cold as a corpse" the DBT patient later revealed. The sight of her upset the borderline patient because it reminded her that she, too, was back in the hospital. It also made her take a hard, realistic look at the ravages of anorexia nervosa.

When she returned to the BPD unit, crying so hard that she could barely breathe, she waved away all the nurses and PAs who approached. She then sat down on the bathroom floor and continued her hysterical crying. The thought of belly breathing entered her mind, which she admitted to Dr. Barley seemed ridiculous and totally irrelevant to the crisis situation. She recalled saying out loud to herself, "Okay, you've had all this idiotic breathing and relaxation stuff shoved down your throat, let's see you use it." A few minutes later, after using the slower breathing, her crying stopped. She was able to think about what had upset her so terribly, wash her face, and let the nurses know she was all right. "Hey," she thought, "This stuff works!" This Highland patient and P. have something in common in their first response to DBT and their slow assimilation of the skills. But both, too, reached the point of great success using those skills.

One of the first Emotion Regulation Skills is identifying and labeling emotions. Sometimes this alone takes the power away from the emotion. Next, the patient learns to Identify Obstacles to Changing Emotions. Linehan has found that emotions in general operate for two reasons: to communicate to others and to motivate one's own behavior. Linehan also noted that an emotion allows us to influence and control other people's behavior.

Perhaps Kim wants her children to visit her more often while she is hospitalized. She might feel a powerful need to cry in their presence to express her emotion. Perhaps she hopes to make them feel guilty and visit more often. All of this can and usually does take place on an unconscious level. Therefore, Kim's ability to identify and label her emotion as sadness and abandonment might help her to make her children's next visit a happy, positive experience. Being able to do this might help her change her old pattern and influence her children to visit more often.

A lifestyle change called Reducing Vulnerability to "Emotion Mind" is taught next. This change can go a long way toward strengthening an individual emotionally. For example, following a healthy diet, getting enough sleep, exercising, avoiding non-prescribed drugs, increasing mastery—finding something you enjoy doing (sewing, golfing, ironing, writing, babysitting, etc...) and fitting all of that into some sort of regular part of your life can go a long way toward increasing your feelings of competence and self-worth.

Increasing Positive Emotional Events is the next skill. An important way to control emotions is to control the "prompting" events (those that trigger your negative emotions). For this to work, you need to be on your toes. Unfortunately, you might not recognize those triggering events until you are already upset. The instant you find yourself in a situation that negatively affects your emotions, start using the skills best aimed at stopping those emotions. If this fails, belly breathe through the event and tell someone on staff as soon as possible that you've identified an important prompting event.

If seeing her soon-to-be ex-husband was too much for Peggy, then limiting his visits was a good step. Asking for a pass to go to lunch with a fellow patient or visiting family might be a way to increase a positive experience for Peggy. Linehan says that in the long-term individuals will need to make life changes so that positive events occur more often. For some people this means joining a bridge club, going to church, taking a volunteer job, or doing something else that is enjoyable and of value *to them*.

Increasing Mindfulness to Current Emotions is a way to go on and experience the emotions without judging them. This is similar to the example under the Mindfulness skill section—self-talk through an emotion using mindfulness and observation as tools to get through it. For example, I feel tears; they taste like salt; I cry when I am sad; my stomach is rumbling; I feel hunger; dinner is going to be served soon. This type of experience can get one through periods of intense emotionality without the consequence of self-harm.

Doing the Opposite is another emotion regulation skill. One way to deal with an unpleasant emotion is to express an opposing emotion that can eventually take the place of the unpleasantness. For example, Rachel feels tendencies to isolate herself from others. She has learned over time that this can be dangerous for her. Therefore, she resists the urge to stay at home and not answer calls. She has a support network and often calls a friend and invites him or her out. More subtle applications of this skill can be turning a frown of worry into a half-smile, or listening to upbeat music that the individual knows makes them want to whistle or sing aloud when, at the moment, they might feel like avoiding any noise—a total isolation of sorts.

Interpersonal Effectiveness

For the module on Interpersonal Effectiveness Skills, Dr. Barley uses a lot of role-playing during class. One of the most important aspects of interpersonal effectiveness is deciding what you want out of an interaction with another person and planning your conversation ahead of time to prepare to meet that goal. Three basic things come from such interactions: achieving your goal (what you ask for), getting what you want and keeping the relationship on smooth ground, or getting what you want and maintaining your self-esteem.

The first example is easy to visualize. You have a meeting set up with your boss and you want to ask for a raise. Achieving your goal is the most important thing you wish to gain from the interaction. The second example may arise when a husband and wife have two completely different ideas for a vacation. He wants to raft down the Andes; she wants to sunbathe in Cancun. She may ask him to consider her idea or she may offer a compromise, such as white water rafting in Mexico for two days, followed by a weekend at a resort. If her husband remains rigid, she eventually gives in because her main goal in the interaction is to keep the relationship smooth. In the third example, a daughter might ask her parents if she can stay at home while they go on vacation for the weekend. They want her to stay with friends, but she feels she is old enough to be responsible on her own. She asks, but if she meets with resistance, she, too, eventually backs down, knowing she stated her own belief in her self-reliance, and that she was fair to herself and her parents, thereby boosting her self-esteem.

Linehan notes that borderline individuals have a tendency to alternate between avoidance of conflict and intense confrontation, depending upon the individual's emotion state at the time. This does not lend itself well to using the right set of skills for each priority: objective, relationship, self-esteem.

The way to ask for something in each of these interchanges is easy to remember if you use the acronym DEAR MAN—Describe, Explain, Assert, Reinforce, Mindfully, Appear (confident), and Negotiate. Dr. Barley helps DBT participants come up with real-life issues and then role-plays with them, listening for each component of the DEAR format.

The broken-record technique is often used for reinforcement. This is when someone repeats his or her intentions, until the other person understands or communication comes to a close. For example:

Daughter: "Mom, I am sixteen and responsible enough to be home alone for one weekend."

Mother: "No."

Daughter: "I baby-sit other people's children and even handle crises such as Joey's fall. I had to drive him to the emergency room for stitches and keep him calm. You praised my self-reliance then."

Mother: "We said no."

Daughter: "I will keep the Smith's phone number on the refrigerator door and call them if I need anything. I think that's a better arrangement than staying at their house. They aren't inconvenienced and I have a chance to study and prove my responsibility level."

Mother: "Our word is final. No."

Daughter: "Ok. I understand your concerns. But, I hope you've listened to my examples of how responsible I've been. I have a good track record."

In this case, both the parents and the daughter have used the broken record technique. However, the daughter calmly got in the last word. And, that's an important factor. Her belief in her ability to be responsible is the last thing stated in the interaction and the last words normally are remembered longest. Linehan's acronym for self-respect interchanges is DEAR MAN GIVE—which gives the additional skills of being Gentle, Interested, Validate, and using an Easy manner.

When the relationship is the highest priority in an interchange the acronym DEAR MAN FAST can help individuals remember to be Fair, offer no Apologies, Stick to values, and be Truthful.

SUMMARY

✦ *The concept of the "wise mind"—the balance between intellect and emotion—is presented in DBT.*

✦ *Mindfulness—being aware of emotions but non-judgmental towards them—is taught first.*

✦ *Emotion Regulation Skills include:*
  Identify Obstacles to Changing Emotions
  Reducing Vulnerability to "Emotion Mind"
  Increasing Positive Emotional Events
  Increasing Mindfulness to Current Emotions
  Doing the Opposite

✦ *Interpersonal Effectiveness Skills:*

Your priority is:	*These skills apply:*	
Achieving	Describe	Mindfully
your goal	Explain	Appear (confident)
	Assert	Negotiate
	Reinforce	
Maintaining	D M	Gentle
your self-respect	E A	Interested
	A N	Validate
	R	using an Easy manner
Maintaining	D M	Fair
the relationship	E A	offer no Apologies
	A N	Stick to values
	R	be Truthful.

Chapter 6

◖ USING ALL THE TRICKS OF THE TRADE

D istress Tolerance is the final module in Linehan's skills training. It is a form of reality acceptance in that borderline individuals can expect to feel really awful at times. Distress tolerance also means you can get through to the other side of feeling awful. "DBT assumes that most people, including borderline individuals, feel badly for good reasons," (Linehan). This is a very validating and important approach to those with borderline personality disorder. The individuals suffering from this are not play acting or manipulative on a conscious level. Yet, some therapists even shy away from treating those with borderline personality for such reasons.

At a recent meeting of mental health professionals, P. saw this attitude first-hand. She was shocked and looked to her doctors who shared her amazement as a mental health professional discussed the manipulative, promiscuous behavior of borderlines in general, based on his experience with one patient. Furthermore, DBT-embracing mental health professionals saw the cry for help in this patient's actions. It made P. and others listening to this particular paper long to erase the stigma attached not only to mental illness in general but to borderline personality in particular. DBT validates patients' behaviors, and then works to replace ineffective, maladaptive behaviors with the skills that can help the individual lead a life worth living.

When Isabelle thinks of her illness an analogy a dear friend gave her comes to mind. This friend had a horrible case of poison ivy and felt he was going to literally jump out of his skin. He related this to Isabelle who agreed that's how she felt when her emotions were raging. "But", he said, "I know I'm going to get over this outbreak and I'm equally sure I will get poison ivy again." "I was touched by how well he understood my feelings. So, when I feel really down, I pick up my own 'calamine' lotion—DBT skills—and prepare to feel badly for a while with the assurance that I *will* feel better again. In the back of my mind I know I will feel badly again—but that's where DBT comes in. Feeling badly is not so scary when I know I *can* and *do* get through such emotional turbulence. After all, my friend won't forego the woods he loves for fear of poison ivy; nor will I forego meeting new experiences, taking new risks and just living for fear of a difficult emotional state."

Among the distress tolerance skills is the skill of distraction. In some ways this is the opposite of mindfulness in that a person works to take their mind off the distressing emotion(s). Each individual has different distracting skills. For some it is reading. Others, who find intense concentration impossible at some moments, might look through the pictures of a magazine, or take a long walk. Exercise is a wonderful distraction. Games, such as the oft-mentioned Scrabble® game can also turn the mind away from other thoughts. Self-soothing is an important part of distraction. Linehan notes that for many borderline individuals these skills are difficult to use because they do not feel worthy of caring. Yet, warm baths with lots of bubbles and a good magazine in hand, a favorite lotion, putting on an attractive outfit—appealing to the five senses can be an effective distraction, and quite pleasant once an individual has the skills in hand. A change in physiology is often recommended—if you're hot, take a cold shower—if you're agitated, the warm bath might be better. There are as many healthy core skills from which to choose as you can imagine. Kim distracts with word search games, often going through an entire book of them in an evening.

Remember Dr. Peterson's advice about learning to be comfortable with a new golf grip as a way to explain that you should hold a piece of ice rather than a razor blade? This technique should be used when the urge hits to cut or otherwise engage in self-harm. Ice, held in the hand or applied to the wrists until the entire arm aches can bring relief to a person who wants to feel pain. No permanent damage is done, and the urge subsides, sometimes within the period of time it takes for the ice to melt. One patient mentioned that ice on her wrists brought out the scars there, showing them in vivid purple, reminding her how much pain she had caused herself and those who care about her and how badly she wishes to erase that pain. The ice is particularly effective for her. Knitting and other crafts, listening to or playing music, playing with a favorite pet, talking to a friend about enjoyable things, watching a comedy on television

and more can distract a person from painful, self-puni-
tive emotions.

Peggy has come a long way in her months at
Highland. She has learned to stand up for herself rather
than be beaten down by words of others, even her
husband. Her doctors agree that it is her relationship
with her husband and his unrealistic expectations that
has brought on her deep depression. He has been unrelenting during visits, even during meetings with Peggy
and her therapist and social worker. He refuses any of
the things Peggy has requested, continuing to believe that
her illness does not require doctors or medicine, but
merely "bootstrap" therapy. His attitude and behavior
invalidates the real pain involved and the difficulty in
getting better. It's time for interpersonal effectiveness and
reality acceptance. For Peggy this means ending a hope-
less relationship. She plans to file for divorce and custody
of their three daughters. She knows it will be an uphill
battle and an emotional roller-coaster, but the thought
of returning to the battleground she left as one of the
walking wounded is an unacceptable alternative.

"I refuse to go backwards. I've made it this far. I'm
alive and able to find a ray of sunshine even on the cloudi-
est days. I have my health back. I love my children. And,
whatever happens, I *will* have my self-esteem intact." For
the treatment team and patients who have known Peggy,
this will is beautiful to see. Fellow patients describe her
as having grown more vertebrae—she's got spine!

In her book, *Stronger Than Death: When Suicide Touches
Your Life,* Dr. Sue Chance states that "insight without
action is fruitless." A tenet of behavior therapists is that
behavior change leads to emotional and cognitive
changes. That is one way of stating the need for distress

tolerance. Chance had to come to terms with her son's suicide. As a psychiatrist, she had keen insight that often seemed to make that terrible task even more difficult. Every suicide survivor asks why?, but Chance asked, "Why didn't I see the signs sooner?" Yet, she painfully and powerfully learned that it was her son and not she or anyone else who ultimately was responsible for what took place. However all of her insight would be useless, she notes, if she did not go forward and do something with that insight. That is an example of distress tolerance and reality acceptance to the core!

Dr. Linehan puts it this way: If a circumstance is causing you pain, change the circumstance. If the circumstance is unchangeable, change your response to the circumstance. Applying this, look at Peggy's situation again. Her marriage is causing her extreme pain. She has tried everything she and her doctors know to attempt counseling with her husband and other means to obtain a circumstance where she could not just survive but thrive. "He gives everything he has of himself to his job. He bows down to the god of the almighty dollar at the expense of our marriage and seeing his beautiful daughters growing up!" Peggy asks him if he loves her, and he says "No. I married you because you wanted to get married." The circumstance is not going to change. But, Peggy can, with a heavy emotional price, change her circumstance. She can get out of the marriage.

What about a person who is miserable in a job that is unchallenging yet necessary to pay the bills? This person is reliant on the medical insurance used to alleviate the mental distress created by the job. Every day he or she goes into the office, loses more self-esteem, and feels as if a grave of depression is being dug. The person looks at alternatives. No jobs are available; there's a recession on and people say, "feel lucky you have a job at all at the rate the company has been laying people off." So, panic strikes. The person decides to hold onto the job even though there are severe problems with it.

What if people in this position use some distress tolerance? They can't for the moment change their circumstance, but they can change their response to it. They can say to themselves each morning, "this is just a job." I'll go in and work my eight hours and then I'll be free to do the things I care about most in life. Then, they proceed to discover those things that bring them the most joy and contentment—playing softball, volunteering time at a nursing home, reading books. They schedule their time so that they can do these things more often, using the time they have after and even before work. They find they no longer are chained to the job. They see it as only one part of an active, healthy, relatively content lifestyle. When people ask them what they do (meaning, of course for a living), they might even answer "Oh, lots of things." No longer do they identify themselves with a single unhappy aspect of their life because their use of distress tolerance has brought relief and personal freedom.

In some cases distress tolerance means accepting the seemingly intolerable for a period of time. When Sue Chance's son died, the pain she felt was excruciating. When Kim's father died, her loss felt unbearable. Kim and her husband also fostered over ten children, who they grew to love and cherish, only to lose them to permanent, adoptive parents. "That felt like death every time," Kim says. And, when Isabelle's mother committed suicide, she thought she'd never be able to stop crying again. But, these individuals did it. They lived through the worst thing they could imagine and came through on the other side of the eclipse.

Sometimes self-talk is helpful in these extreme situations. "I'm alive. I'm standing up. This hasn't killed me. I'm going to make it through the next ten minutes." Yes, sometimes it means breaking life down into nanoseconds and believing you can get through at least the next few. Tolerance of the moment is the DBT lexicon for this skill—maybe "tolerance of the nanosecond" is appropriate in some cases. For, that's what Isabelle finds herself doing when the urge to hurt herself comes to the fore.

Many try to make a schedule and stick to it. If that schedule includes things like buying a book (distraction), going for walks (change in physiology, distraction and self-soothing), splurging on an occasional rose for myself (self-soothing, imagery—appealing to touch, sight and smell), on these days, the borderline is using the newly learned skills well.

Tolerating distress means taking all of your skills and aiming the appropriate one(s) at the pain. Most often *something* works. Remember your crisis intervention skills, too. You can call your therapist and/or 911. Your goal is to make it through your most awful moments when the eclipse of darkness seems to surround you and block any possibility of the sun shining again on your tear-stained face. You can achieve your goal and dispel the darkness with an overall understanding of the skills you've gained and what works for you.

No one skill or set of skills works for every patient. It is up to the patient, with help from the therapist, to practice the skills and learn what works and in what order it works best. Practicing the skill of the Pros and Cons, that is weighing all the positive results from not committing self-harm against all the negative results, is a powerful skill for most patients. However, it doesn't always, or often, work, if it is the first skill tried. Lowering your emotional level to a point where you can concentrate on these points is often required. In DBT class at Highland, Dr. Barley points out that the material he is going over may or may not work, depending on you and/or the circumstance. Linehan strongly backs this up. "Credibility is damaged when leaders promise that a particular skill will solve a particular problem. In fact, DBT is something of a shotgun approach: Some of the skills work some of the time for some of the people. I have not had clients to date who could not benefit from something, but no one benefits from everything."

Borderlines find themselves "awfulizing" many situations. "I lost my job. This is the worst thing that could ever happen to me!" Is it really? It's bad. It's frightening. It requires some rethinking and planning. But, they also can say, "I'm alive. I have a loving family. I have a strong faith. I have the best darned cat anyone could hope to have," or whatever fits the case. Then, they can look back at the real worst thing that ever happened to them. "I almost killed myself a year ago, and today I have a wonderful baby son. I need a new job, but the worst thing would be for me not to have been here to bring that precious boy into this world. I made it through that, we'll make it through this." Distress tolerance is powerful medicine.

A diary card of DBT skills is given to individuals in class. They are expected to track which skills they use and when. This seems awkward at first, but might become second nature before too long. Practice, practice, and more practice is crucial to the successful use of skills. The diary card is a wonderful way to determine which skills work, and under what circumstances. With this basic sketch of skills in mind, it might seem hard to understand why failure occurs at times. Sometimes patients fail to use their skills; other times the skills they choose are not helpful in addressing their level of distress. Sometimes patients simply can't get through a certain distressing feeling or urge without intervention by others. If the person fails to recognize this level of distress, parasuicide can occur. Sometimes skills haven't been practiced sufficiently. Sometimes the patient fails to "turtle" and acts impulsively. A system is set in place to keep the patient focused on using their skills, once appropriate medical attention has been applied.

Protocols

Highland and Cornell Medical Center, Westchester Division require a formal procedure drawn from DBT when a self-harmful urge is acted upon by a patient. The Highland model is adapted from one developed by Charles Swenson, M.D. of Cornell, now in private practice and Medical Director of Mental Health Programs in Western Massachusetts.

Isabelle did not use her distress tolerance skills when the fact that she was back in the hospital weighed heavily upon her. She used to joke about this with her doctors and other patients, saying "Yeah, I'm a recidivist." Not this night. She felt like a failure. The image of a husband who loved her and stood by her through her illness dimmed as she imagined he would be so much better off without her. As a suicide survivor herself, she should have known better. But, during this dark hour, she forgot. She plugged up the sink and attempted to drown herself. During checks, she was found. She tried desperately to lock the bathroom door against the PA who pushed his way in. His words to her were so meaningful, that they got through her fuzzy thinking. Their conversation ran something like this:

"What's bothering you?"

"Look at me! What do you see? A DBT Flunkout! Don't you see a failure?!"

"No," he quietly answered very dialectically, "I see a survivor."

A *survivor!* Isabelle had been trying to look at things in black and white again: I'm either a success or a failure; I'm a failure; I should die. Wrong-headed thinking can lead to dreadfully wrong actions. She and her skills had failed in the crisis. Her logic was off-course. It needed to be nudged back on course, and so it was.

"Maybe the opposite of success isn't failure," she said to the aide, "maybe it's survival." He'd gotten through to her. Better, still, she had pulled through the crisis.

"You're going to have to do a protocol on this you know."

They both laughed a little at that. The dreaded protocol seemed a small price to pay for what she had learned.

For the time immediately following any parasuicidal action (not less than two hours), the patient is required to remain in view of the nurse's station while filling out paperwork on the event. A form with questions about the internal and external triggers of the emotions, your thoughts about those emotions and what action/urges you had is to be completed. In other words, the protocol is filled out to let people know what you were feeling, what you thought about those feelings and what you did about it. The rest of the paperwork is more detailed. The patient needs to identify what skills they tried to put in place to avoid the incident, and then come up with a plan for avoiding such an incident in the future. The patient then needs to repair any relationships that may have been strained by the parasuicidal behavior. This usually involves calling a meeting of as many patients as possible on the DBT unit. The meeting must be witnessed by at least two professionals, a nurse and psychiatric aide, in most cases. Then the paperwork is verbally accounted to the group and apologies are made to anyone upset by the actions.

It is amazing how useful these events can be, even though the DBT patients dread these gatherings—the "dreaded Protocol, indeed." However, to hear that so-and-so tried to kill herself last night through the rumor mill is not only demeaning to the patient involved but damaging to the milieu. The protocol places the facts of the situation up front. Isabelle's closest friends on the unit gave her hell for not talking to them or someone before she did this. Peggy was most outspoken, letting her know that she was hurt personally because she thought their friendship was stronger than Isabelle's behavior seemed to credit it. Apologies were made and Isabelle rightly identified the fact that she tends to get most upset in the evenings and should not isolate herself in her room during that time. If she had been out in the lounge, she probably would have talked with Peggy about her feelings of failure rather than ruminating on them until she took action.

The protocol is then reviewed with the patient by the

therapist. Suggestions are often added to the plan by the therapist to avoid future incidents. The protocol is signed and placed in the patient's chart.

Safety Plans and Contracts

Patients are encouraged to develop safety plans. A safety plan is a quick reference list of the skills that work best for the patient and to which the patient can refer in a time of distress. As a patient nears discharge, these plans are honed with therapist and other team members' input, based on their observations and knowledge of the individual. Many rely on self-soothing techniques and distraction as their main skills. Some add a list of pros that might include reasons for self-harm (i.e. relief, revenge) and the likely consequences, re-emergence of a higher stress level than before the self-harm, possible death, and anger rather than sympathy by the person or person(s) toward which the revenge was directed. The listing of pros leads to a list of cons or reasons for *not* committing a destructive act. Dr. Barley heavily loads the dice in favor of *not* committing self-harm, tolerating the situation and accompanying emotions.

For some, the cons consist of improving their self-esteem by proving they *can* make it through terrible moments, days, weeks without giving in to their old patterns. Avoidance of hospitalization and the feeling often described as moving five steps forward and six steps backward often sets in. Other cons are recognizing that the revenge sought is not directed toward oneself, but rather toward others, having a chance to process these thoughts with a clear head and gaining a more positive relationship effectiveness skill in order to improve or end relationships that cause so much turmoil.

The list of skills in the order in which they work the most quickly and effectively, becomes the backbone structure of a safety plan. The plan is then fleshed out with built in crisis intervention precautions. No plan is complete without a list of people to call and their phone numbers. This can include understanding friends and relatives, therapists (DBT therapists will take calls between sessions within limits), and emergency personnel at 911. It is essential that the plan address mild, moderate, and extreme distress levels. The plan should be written in simple language on index cards. This will help the individual who is not in a state to concentrate, but to act, comprehend it easily.

Most patients find that the first two or three cards help them through most distressing times. Other times they may need to use the whole stack of cards and even begin again at the top—maybe from turtling to self-soothing to ice holding to voluntarily admitting themselves to the nearest hospital for crisis intervention purposes. Such admissions normally are brief, with the individual returning to a safe state quickly. Sometimes medication adjustments are required, and this need helps explain why the individual went from handling things well to having more difficulties. No patient was discharged from the BPD unit without a solid safety plan in hand.

Contracts are another part of the protocol. They are made between patients and the treatment team or therapist if the person is an inpatient or between the patient and therapist, spouse, family, or self if the person is an outpatient. After an incident of self-harm or recurrent dangerous thought patterns, such contracts are put in place for an agreed upon period of time. The wording can be quite simple, however the contract is considered binding. An inpatient contract can be simply stated and say, "I agree not to engage in parasuicidal behavior and to report urges to do so immediately to staff." The patient would then sign and date this each morning before rounds. This would remain in effect until the team requests its end after determining that the patient's track record was solid and believing she could maintain herself safely without it.

Working with outpatients, Linehan has found the contract system worked well for her patients. However, some patients repeatedly had difficulty with the agreement to call their therapist *before* they committed any self-harmful behavior. This frustrates doctors and often holds therapy back in several ways. Kim often called and said, "I've cut myself, what should I do now?"

Such a breach of contract, however, can and does lead to serious consequences concerning therapists. Some therapists finally have to admit that continual self-harmful patterns are too much for them to handle. Some even remove themselves from a case. "This process is particularly challenging to the clinician's ability and desire to help the patients."[1]

Such a situation could send patients over the emotional edge. But, their therapist can suggest the patient return to a former psychiatrist or therapist, or recommend a new one. They might even find a way to see the patient until they can make arrangements to either return to treatment with them, or find someone else with whom the patient is comfortable to take the case.

DBT therapists try to use a hierarchy of responses to repeated undesirable behaviors: disapproval, correction—overcorrection (e.g., talking the problem to death), protocols, and even putting the patient "on vacation" from treatment, temporarily.

"I realize my responsibility in this. I broke my contract, my word. I'm a difficult patient. I can imagine the doctor needs a break from the case," Kim and others have said dialectically as they note the other side of the coin. That was after much emotional turmoil verging on the point of hysteria.

SUMMARY

⚬ *The skills of distress tolerance aid the borderline in getting through some of the toughest times.*

⚬ *Distraction is a useful skill that includes self-soothing techniques or change in body physiology, such as heavy exercise or a cold shower.*

⚬ *A borderline may learn to use a substitute for self-harm. For example, holding ice cubes on the wrists until pain is experienced may provide some relief as a substitute for cutting.*

⚬ *The skill of Pros and Cons helps to put the positive and negative outcomes of self-harm into perspective.*

⚬ *Not all skills work at all times. A diary card helps a person track which skills were used and how well they worked. It provides a framework for individuals to determine what works best for them.*

⚬ *A safety plan is a list of skills that can be quickly referred to in times of distress.*

Chapter 7

☾ TREATMENTS

Individual and Group Therapy

The first rule of both individual and group therapy is confidentiality. What is said during these sessions is not to be repeated outside of them, unless it is by individual patients who wish to share their own disclosures with someone close, such as a family member. No one else's disclosures can be revealed. At Highland, group therapy took place twice a week, offering several benefits. As you will remember, BPs are caregivers. Often in group sessions they can help another patient hypothetically solve a situation using DBT skills effectively. Then when it's their turn to disclose how things are going with them, they are asked to listen to the advice of their milieu, since many members have shared similar circumstances. It can be an emotional and stressing time for the group, perhaps for the very reason that each participant must step out of care*giver* and move into care*taker* roles. Group therapy on an inpatient basis can also be a time of addressing a group situation, such as the Domino Effect, or a member's failure to participate (if they are present and able to handle this form of feedback). Members can discuss how these things affect them, and sometimes problem-solving is the result.

However, the emotional sensitivity of the borderline individual precludes standard "processing" practices in group therapy, according to several therapists who work with these patients. Because confrontation might be too upsetting to the individual, comments directed toward those types of activities might not be a part of a borderline group therapy session.

It is important to understand the difference between DBT skills training sessions and group therapy. While both are conducted in a group setting, skills training is like a class where modules of DBT are presented and explored. Sometimes role-playing is used to simulate the use of certain skills, especially in the relation effectiveness module. Group therapy, on the other hand, is just that—therapy. It is not a class and is not a time to take notes or approach it in a standard class-like frame of mind. The goal is therapeutic treatment rather than skills training.

The treatment team offers "treatment for the therapist" as an integral part of DBT treatment. In other words, the group meetings by the treatment team can be a time for therapists to receive feedback on whether they are too close to a situation, or whether they are addressing issues with patients dialectically, etc. This type of approach is extremely important for the therapist and other members of the treatment team. They need attention and feedback on where they are "on-track" as do their patients. This is a real strength of the treatment team approach.

Individual therapy is a one-to-one encounter with a patient's therapist. Daunting at first, this may come to be one of the most relaxing and beneficial times of the week for some patients. Problem-solving is a goal. However the warmth and understanding of the therapist undergirds the patient. "I know you are hurting; don't underestimate your loss," and other gentle cheerleading statements can help a patient through even the most overwhelmingly painful times.

Linehan refers to one attitude of "warm ruthlessness" as a dialectical approach, rather than just straight cheerleading when such an attitude might be helpful in moving a person beyond inaction based on "poor me" feelings. Individual therapy follows the hierarchy of stopping self-harm and treatment-interfering behaviors first. If the patient is ready, the hierarchy might move to what is known as stage two issues. Then it might be a time when past experiences are explored, and this excavation can be a stressor that translates into a tumultuous time for the patient before, during, and after sessions. For this very reason, DBT patients stay in stage one of the hierarchy for as long as necessary. Because current prompting events prompt current distress, in the lexicon of a behavior therapist, it is critical that the patient fully address stage one issues first.

Prompting Events

Once a patient moves on to stage two, usually talking through and facing past trauma lays the groundwork for understanding current prompting events. The effect of facing their trauma, however, can be devastating to the emotionally vulnerable individual not prepared for stage two therapeutic approaches. If this is the case, it is critical that the therapist and patient discuss this effect. Dr. Peterson repeatedly uses the phrase "pace yourself." A patient and therapist may be making tremendous progress identifying traumas that cause current distress. However, the pace at which these traumas are explored can be adjusted to the patient's level of skillful acceptance and problem-solving abilities.

Electro-Convulsive Therapy (ECT)

In severe cases of unrelenting depression, ECT might be considered. Kim and Peggy both underwent a series of these treatments while at Highland. The procedure is given under general anesthesia, and the heart and brain functions are monitored during the process. The rationale behind the treatment is that something is blocking normal brain activity, and carefully controlled amounts of electricity administered can change the current brain activity slightly in order to remove the blockage. The main side effect of this therapy is mild memory loss, which clinicians agree usually lasts a maximum of two to six months. Directly after the procedure, patients sometimes complain of severe headaches, which are treated with pain medication. Both Peggy and Kim were up and dressed for the day after having treatments early in the morning. However, both complain of continuing memory loss.

"I have things in my closet that I don't recognize." Kim says. "I asked my husband where these things came from, because they aren't to my taste. I was astonished when he told me that I had purchased these things. I would never wear red stirrup pants!" Kim laughs a little when she says this, but she emphasizes that it really isn't funny to her. "It's been over a year, and I still have things I can't recall clearly. I know this treatment works for some people, but I haven't met anyone who doesn't complain about the residual memory loss," she adds.

Dr. Barley clarifies that such an experience clearly could be a dissociative episode rather than memory loss. In fact in most cases of this nature the patient experiences dissociative or another disorder. ECT is rarely the culprit.

Peggy was terrified of going under general anesthesia. "I know it seems ironic that a suicidal person would be so scared of dying under the anesthesia. But, I guess that just wasn't my choice of a way to go out. I felt totally out of control of the procedure and was absolutely certain I would never wake up." She voiced her fears to her closest friends on the unit. Each morning when she had a treatment scheduled (they are generally administered in a series of 10 to 12 over a period of weeks), one of those friends would be outside her door, ready to hold her hand all the way to the treatment room. Isabelle gave Peggy a guardian angel pin to wear. Of course she couldn't have any jewelry on during the ECT, so, she pinned it to her hospital gown, and a kind nurse would take it off and wear it where Peggy could see it until the anesthesia took effect.

"That was such a gentle and kind gesture. It made things easier, especially since my husband, who knew how afraid I was, came for only one treatment. I couldn't believe his lack of support. I had to look for it in other places, and miraculously it came—from patients and staff, alike. I may have some memory loss, but I'll never forget that support," Peggy says.

Although Peggy and Kim did not feel they gained significant relief from depression through ECT, others noticed a difference in their levels of motivation and in other areas. Further, doctors have witnessed cases where the patient did gain tremendous relief from just a few treatments. Although undergoing any procedure requiring general anesthesia is not without risk, ECT has come a long way in recent years, has shown positive, life-saving results, and remains an option for psychiatry. This section would not be complete without the caveat that ECT, especially several series of the treatment, can cause some amount of brain damage. If your doctor believes you are a candidate for this therapy, conduct your own research and make an educated decision. Kim firmly believes that results should be noticeable after one series. "If they aren't, I personally would not agree to go on with the treatment. That, of course, is my own belief. Others should make their own choices about this course of treatment."

Dr. William Barley actually has seen cases where ECT *has saved lives* and strongly urges considering it as an option if it is recommended by your doctors.

Medication (Adjustments and Management)

Not all borderline patients are treated with medication; however, a large number of them are on antidepressants. Once the depression is lifted, the need for other medications can be determined and/or adjusted by the attending physician. According to Dr. Peterson, most if not all borderlines suffer from depression. He said that he had yet to see a case of untreated BPD where the patient was not in a depressed state.

The literature on pharmaco-therapy of BPD is becoming increasingly sophisticated. Most psychiatrists recommend treating BPD target symptoms "rationally"—using the wise mind. That is they prescribe antidepressants for depression;

antiolytics for anxiety and fear; mood stabilizers for mood instability, etc.

Other medications may be aimed at treating panic or anxiety attacks, sleeplessness, impulsive behavior, and other symptoms. All medications need to be monitored to ensure they are in an effective therapeutic level in the patient's bloodstream. Some medications are toxic in large doses and are monitored more frequently. This may mean regular blood tests and requires a knowledgeable physician acquainted with the side effects of and purposes for these specialized medications. A psychiatrist often is the best choice for medication management and adjustment decisions. It can be part of your regular therapy to discuss any suspected side effects or difficulties, and brief hospitalizations to resolve these problems might take place from time to time.

Some research indicates that a few medications might create less inhibition in borderline patients. Hostility and impulsivity have been seen to increase in borderlines on certain medications. This is not a wide-spread result; however, it warrants careful attention by the patient and medication management physician alike.

Once patients discontinue therapy, they may continue to see a psychiatrist annually or on a schedule arranged for medication management and/or adjustments as required. Sometimes a patient can be taken off medication. However, this can be a complex process, especially if the patient is on several different medications. Weaning and careful monitoring by the physician is important during this time. Patients who start feeling better, may rashly decide to discontinue their medication cold turkey. This is not advisable and could result in serious side effects. This caveat is serious. Not working honestly with your doctor to manage medication change can be fatal.

Crisis Intervention

Discharge plans for Highland patients include crisis intervention planning. Should the outpatient become suicidal or distressed to a level that is not safe for themselves or others, they need to know what to do. Often keeping a series of numbers close by (on the patient or near the telephone—whatever works!) is the first step. Perhaps this could begin with calling a friend or family member familiar with your disorder and discussing possible skills to use. If this call fails, or if the people on the list are not available, a crisis line can be used. Trained counselors can direct you to call your doctor, use certain techniques known to help in your situation, or determine if you need to be hospitalized.

Asheville doctors treating the borderline individual require that partial hospital, intensive outpatient, and outpatient individuals *must* be in phone contact with their primary therapists in times of crises. Should the therapeutic relationships be strained between these patients and their therapists, other persons might be called during crises—*if* this has been agreed to by the patient and therapist very early in treatment. However, the individual's therapist remains the patients' primary contact when/if their own contact persons are insufficient.

Former inpatients often have a tremendous fear of being re-hospitalized. They might think it marks a big failure on their part to reintegrate into the real world. Or, they might recall the length of their last stay and fear such a long stay would be necessary again. However, crisis intervention stays are almost always brief and are directed at getting the patient back on track and into the outpatient realm as quickly as is safe. Sometimes it is a simple medication adjustment that is necessary; sometimes it is simply an overnight stay in a controlled environment for safety. If the patient has returned to work outside the home, they might be afraid of losing their job if they require further hospitalization. But a quick crisis intervention stay can be covered easily by sick days or an honest discussion with a supervisor who understands the situation.

As for thinking re-hospitalization is a failure, dialectical thinking (looking at both sides of an issue) is required. This is a success! Learning to take care of yourself, using every skill and resource you have is the name of the game. Think of re-hospitalization as preventive medicine that you have taken on your own. You are not out of control, but have your situation well in hand. Give yourself a pat on the back. Family members and friends need to understand the importance of crisis intervention and their role (if any) in it. They should also know that validation of your actions is important.

SUMMARY

◈ *Individual therapy, in conjunction with DBT, follows the same hierarchy as DBT: stopping self-harm first, then addressing behavior that interferes with treatment.*

◈ *Group therapy offers the advantage that participants can give support and feedback to each other.*

◈ *Unlike therapy, the goal of DBT is the learning of skills rather than therapeutic treatment.*

◈ *Electro-Convulsive Treatment (ECT)* **has saved lives.**

◈ *Medication alone or with psychotherapy can be effective.*

Chapter 8

❨ FAMILY RELATIONSHIPS

Validation within a hospital or therapy setting is important. However, if the patient's significant others are not educated about the concept of validation, a lot of hard work can be destroyed. The other pole of the overarching dialectic of "problem-solving" requires family support. The doctors, therapies, medications, and hard-working individuals make up the other pole—that can't stand alone.

A supportive, educated family or friend(s) can be, quite literally a lifeline, for a patient suffering BPD. It is unrealistic to expect the world to change to fit the borderline's sensitivities. Indeed, change on the part of the borderline is of paramount importance. However, if the borderline can find a source of validation, especially during initial treatment and difficult times thereafter, the success rate in treatment dramatically improves.

Supportive Behaviors

Peggy was discharged from the hospital and returned to her parents' home rather than to the home she and her husband shared prior to her inpatient treatment. Her mother and father exhibited extremely supportive behavior, and continue to be helpful in innumerable ways.

"They help when I have the girls on the weekends. Dad bought a computer and paid for classes to help me get motivated and prepared for a career since everything seems to require computer-literacy these days. I'm more than grateful for their attitude and strong shoulders."

Peggy's mother experienced depression during the years after her third child was born. At that time she received ECT treatments much less sophisticated than the treatments to which Peggy submitted. Perhaps this brush with mental illness, treatment, and wellness as much as anything else, accounts for Peggy's supportive family.

As serious as Kim's suicide attempts continue to be, and as deep down as her depression brings her, her husband has stood firmly by her side. "Why do you put up with this?" she asks from time to time. "I'm not the same person you married. You never bargained for this." Kim gets tears in her eyes when she says, "he just smiles and says, 'I'm going to wait for her to come back to me. I know she will.'"

Kim isn't as optimistic as her husband is, but she appreciates her husband's support. They have four children, all of whom can be more than a little demanding and draining at times. They cared for several foster children in the earlier days of their marriage and in a sense Kim still mourns the loss of those children, even while she faces the challenges of her family life. The strongest tie that seems to hold the whole thing together is Kim's faith. She gets into modes when she wants to join her father in heaven, then her abhorrence of suicide seems to wrangle within her. It's time for a word search puzzle or other distraction.

She keeps on going. It's very rewarding to receive a letter from her, because she is so understanding and kind. Her family values really pour out as do her caring and sense of responsibility. Like Isabelle, she wonders if her family would be better off without her. Isabelle was quick to remind her in the hospital that it was her own mother's death that greatly contributed to Isabelle's illness.

"I hate you," Kim says with a smile. "I know you do, because you know I'm right," Isabelle answers. Another Positron and Negatron, perhaps?

NON-SUPPORTIVE BEHAVIORS

Non-Understanding Behaviors

Isabelle describes her father's initial attitude toward her illness as a lack of understanding. Let's face it, the illness is complex.

For Isabelle, this meant adopting an ability to sit still and wait and try to be the "good girl" so that she could avoid one of the land mines home life represented. Her alcoholic father and sometimes drug-experimenting brothers made these real enough land mines.

"Blaming"

Although her parents support her as much as possible, Peggy faces her non-supportive husband who complains about her medical bills and continues to tell her she just needs to get a "real job." Until she went through months of intensive treatment at Highland, she couldn't say what she really believes: raising three children *is* a full-time job!

Comparison/Denigration/Bootstrap Therapy

"Just think if you had a real illness, like cancer or kidney disease. You're plenty healthy, you just need to get out into the community and interact with people in the real world," Peggy's husband declared so often it became a litany of their life together. "Now, I do compare myself with others, and I'm proud of the progress I've made. There are always going to be those more unfortunate than I am, and I count my blessings every night before I go to sleep. This marriage wasn't one of those blessings, but these three girls are. I'm making it just fine, one day at a time, sometimes one minute at a time. But, it's always him who pushes the wrong buttons with me. I seem to handle confrontation and disappointments in other areas of my life, well, dialectically. I see the silver lining in the dark cloud," Peggy says. "I look for it."

When I was hospitalized initially in my home-town, my husband and I expected a discharge before Christmas. My husband ran interference with friends and family, not letting them know where I was. That wasn't easy with the holiday approaching and both sides of the family trying to plan get-togethers. But, I was terrified of the impact I would have on my father and he on me since we had been through my own mom's five-year struggle with and final defeat by depression.

Finally, there was no getting around the fact that I would be in the hospital through the holidays and was likely to be referred to Highland which was further from home. My husband broke the news, and I faced Dad during a visit for the first time. He was so supportive. I told him I honestly expected him to tell me to pull myself up by my bootstraps, even though they'd taken my shoe laces away, as a suicide precaution. That really got to him. He saw that there was some spark of humor in me still. My brother flew in from California, another offered to come on the next flight from Dallas—an offer I wish I'd accepted. That brother died of a heart attack two months later. I think that had a lot to do with my deepening depression. When it rains, it pours."

—*MFT*

Inconvenience/Embarrassment/Taboo

For Emily, her husband's unsupportive nature toward her illness became dangerous. He told her that her doctors had no idea what was good for her and asked, then demanded, that she get off all medication. Emily agreed, as much to appease him as to see if she would feel better without medication. "It was a bad experiment," Emily recalls. "It literally just about did me in. He may be embarrassed by this, and I had to face that same kind of taboo at work, until I went on disability. But, I'm back on my medicine, and he no longer tries to play the doctor in the house."

SUMMARY

↬ *Supportive family members and friends can play a vital role in the success of a borderline's treatment.*

↬ *Non-supportive behaviors that impede the borderline's progress can include:*
- Invalidating remarks
- Excessive blaming
- "Bootstrap therapy", i.e., "Just pull yourself up by your bootstraps."
- Underestimating the seriousness of the disorder

How I Feel Today

Alone.
So alone.
I feel so alone deep inside.
This feeling grows
and creeps up on me.

Like vines growing up
and around. There is
this wall made to protect me
from what?
I am not sure.
It's encompassing, it's smothering,

Stretching cruelly all around me.
as the vines begin to wrap around me;
so tight they start to choke me.
The days go by so slowly.
The nights are frightening and
broken by bad dreams
that haunt me…
Alone.
Alone and caught in this feeling.
There's no one to cut these vines
these vines that choke me
no one to soothe the hurt
I feel inside.
Alone…

"Rachel"
September 18, 1986

Chapter 9

❨ RECOVERY: THE HELL OF GETTING WELL

Ironically, returning from the darkness of depression and using new skills to cope with BPD can be a frightening and dangerous process. It seems like a paradox, but letting go of an illness means all those expectations "out there" that have been held at bay come back to the doorstep. For borderlines, expectations of themselves to perform perfectly is hard to set aside, and self-punishment for "failure" is common.

This confrontation with expectations is addressed by Linehan who refers to it as "worry thoughts." Worry thoughts are one of five motivational problems which interfere with skilled behavior. The other four are lack of skill, emotion, indecision (about goals, means of achieving them, etc.), and environment (including non-reinforcing family members).

"We should strive for excellence, but not perfection," Isabelle says. "But, I'm so afraid of not doing everything just right. I mean my family went through hell with me and for me, and I feel I owe them a perfect performance as a wife and worker. It was hard for me to go on disability. I lost my job due to the extended hospital stays, and my outpatient treatment, including medications, makes it hard for us to make ends meet. I felt inadequate because I knew I couldn't handle the demands of a daily job, much less a career because I have days when I still can't seem to get out of bed and function," she adds.

Isabelle's husband continues to provide tremendous support to her. He understands when she doesn't get out one day, and just encourages her to use her skills and reminds her that she might feel entirely different the next day.

"He's right," Isabelle agrees. "I do feel the ebb and flow of emotions. Some days are awful, others are fine, and most are just okay. I need to remember that, because it's a perfect example of dialectical thinking—awful at one end, fine on the other, and okay in the middle."

Skill Maintenance: A New Deck of Cards

We sometimes joke about "playing with a new deck," gently making fun of our own illness, a member of the slumber party admits. We all have our discharge plans on index cards, and we remind one another to use them. The learned skills might appear inadequate for the moment, but remember the patient who was hysterically upset after the worship service where she had seen her anorexic friend? Belly breathing to distraction, to holding ice, to calling your therapist—all are skills worth keeping on hand.

During the slumber party, the former unit cohorts, now people working hard toward wellness, would remind each other about their medication times.

"It was kind of like we were going off like a set of cuckoo clocks," Emily explains with a grin. "In fact that's how we described it, since none of us took the same medication at the same time. It would hurt if someone from the outside, who had never seen the inside of a psychiatric hospital had called us 'cuckoo'—but we had each other then, and we have each other now—and we can laugh about certain things together. That's really important."

Self-Reinforcement

People with BPD must learn to reinforce new behavior themselves. If they backslide and, say, take a mini-overdose of medication "just to get [me] through my father's birthday", they are charged with parasuicidal behavior. Yet in the real world there are no psychiatric assistants to help them process this behavior. To prevent future "slip-ups" the individual must identify potentially dangerous times and learn to make them safe times.

Re-educating family members about the importance of these relatively new skills and associating with new people who will reinforce the skills (such as those in a mental health support group) can be extremely effective. Of course, as part of discharge planning, on-going outpatient therapy with a local doctor is normally required before discharge.

Perhaps someone prone to overdosing should give her medications to a trusted friend or family member to distribute for the weeks before, during, and after a difficult anniversary—such as Kim's father's birthday. When she sails through such a time, she has to give herself an internal gold star—because this is expected behavior. She could reward herself more during the early part of her discharge, but must learn that the real reward is living. For the borderline, survival is a full-time job. People who have not experienced BPD do not understand the significance of this.

Stimulus/Response Generalization

Behavior therapy also emphasizes stimulus generalization and response generalization. These are fancy phrases for applying the new skills in new and different situations and practicing many different skills in response to problem situations.

For example, Kimberly has a dangerous over-dosing track record. In the hospital, she was safe while the medications were given to her by nursing professionals at specific times only. In partial hospitalization, her doctor prescribed enough medication for a week only, and Kim managed this well. But, upon returning home, she felt she answered to no one who truly understood, and she over-dosed. Her outpatient psychiatrist would gladly have given Kim prescriptions in non-lethal amounts had Kim asked. Kim could have generalized her week-at-a-time skills to the unstructured environment of her home.

Kim recognizes the signs of her depression—over-sleeping, missing important appointments, not talking. She relies on the core skill of distraction when these signs appear. Recently, she has been diagnosed with Chronic Fatigue Syndrome, which has complicated her skill maintenance and generalization.

"I used to enjoy word search and crossword puzzles and bury myself in them until I felt safe again. Now, I can't concentrate enough on the puzzles. So, I've substituted listening to music at those times." Yet, this is only one skill, and she needs many in her "toolbox" to increase her safety. Kim *can* maintain her new skills, with practice, practice, practice. Naturally, she must find what works for her and do those things as often and in as many different situations as she can.

Continuing Therapy

Another danger after discharge is the fact that when symptoms begin to disappear, the former patients easily may let down their guard. If they have a rough day at the office or with the kids and don't sleep all night, they think it's normal. If things don't improve, they may return to some or all of the maladjusted coping mechanisms they had used before their treatment. After all, they are returning to a world that is not set up to validate their every emotion. Dr. Barley emphasizes that the continual practice of mindfulness skills, maintenance, and generalization techniques is essential. The durability of new coping skills over time—to the point that they become second nature—is critical, yet extremely difficult for those with BPD.

Keeping a borderline patient in therapy can become a struggle at this point. After hospitalization and intensive submersion in DBT, patients may want to fly on their own, not recognizing the ice on their wings and the low fuel gauge. A crash may be inevitable, as was the case when Emily removed herself from medication without professional consent.

Fear and Anxiety

It's lonely in the real world. Your next door neighbor is not diagnosed with your illness, and won't casually or comfortably discuss your symptoms or strong urges to hurt yourself.

When I returned home from the hospital the first time, I immediately cut my wrists and was returned to that controlled environment. By contrast, when I had completed almost a year of DBT and multiple hospitalizations, my return home involved integrating some things familiar to me from the hospital environment. For example, I continued to drink water from the same cheerful, yellow cup my husband had bought for me during my hospitalization at Highland. Perhaps like a baby with a bottle, it just comforted me. I also continued to sleep under the cotton blanket I had taken to the hospital to make my room more "homey." Now, I was making my home more familiar. The results were positive. I felt more at ease and less alone upon this discharge.

—MFT

Distress Tolerance

As has been mentioned, a big pitfall for the BPD is not remaining in therapy for a sufficient length of time. Linehan notes that borderlines are "notorious" for dropping out of therapy.

"I want to be well *now,* "Isabelle complained the minute she was released from the hospital. She didn't want razors kept from her; she didn't want to go on shopping outings with another person whose job it was to prevent her from buying her former allies of laxatives and diet pills. Her impatience is understandable, but not practical. Isabelle had to develop a safety system to keep her on her toes and using her well practiced skills during difficult times. The last thing she wanted was to see a psychiatrist twice a week, with the stigma and embarrassment she already felt when she explained she had been away because she was ill and hospitalized. What if someone sees her going into the psychiatrist's office? People at church will know. She doesn't want to have a contract with her doctor because she is willing to let go of the obviously parasuicidal behaviors but harbors the desire to lose twenty pounds. Isabelle has to accept that, for her, losing weight is parasuicidal. She may not look in the mirror and see the thin figure everyone else does, but she has to use reality acceptance and "accept" others' perceptions of her. If she begins to lose weight, especially through the use of drugs that can cause serious side effects, she is putting her health, perhaps even her life, in jeopardy.

Dr. Barley noted previously in this book that an early commitment to life is, perhaps, the single best sign a person with BPD will survive.

> I didn't have that early commitment; the odds were against me. Yet, by the time of my release I had written the following confirmation that I was ready to accept my life, look for joy, and go on. I believe in miracles.
>
> *—MFT*

Commitment

I am Committed to this life
of mine
With its sunshine, moonbeams,
rain and thunder.

My life is a gift to me, which
I am beholden to
Protect...even to
Cherish.

This Life of mine I will share
with others—
my talents,
my weaknesses,
my salty tears
my smiles, my fears.

My dreams may come true.
But this is true:
My Life is a gift
I can give to others and
Save for myself...
Like a piece of pie.

Melissa Ford Thornton
1992

Awakening to a Brand New Morning

The slumbering foursome awoke slowly. At first some didn't recognize the surroundings of Kim's house. Then, with smiles, they recalled their slumber party and its success. This was a reunion that might have been depressing, reminding each woman of her time spent in long-term psychiatric care. Yet, it became a touchstone for them—a reminder that they are not alone with the powerful emotions that once controlled their lives. They have soul-mates. Peggy still wears her guardian angel pin. Kim still relies on these women to help her regain important memories. She shows them a beautiful plaque with an encouraging saying inscribed on its surface. "Who gave me this?"

"I did," Peggy says quietly. Peggy knows what it is like to knit together memories that have dimmed.

Isabelle hugs Kim and Emily tightly and makes them promise to stay in touch. She leaves pretty writing paper on Kim's bed and a thank you note, hoping she will find a letter from her in her mailbox one day in the not too distant future. She will.

Emily gathers up her Raggedy Ann doll and promises to stay in touch. Not just with the two who are packing up and heading to their homes, but with herself. It's a promise these women will do their best to hold her to— because they were there and because they care. The sun does shine again, as it is doing brightly on this day. There is no Eclipse at this moment for these friends.

❨ A WORD ON THE REPRESSION RAGE

The concept of repressed memories has come under scrutiny in some quarters and under downright attack in others. Repression means forgetting some memories below the conscious level. In cases of sexual abuse, a person might "remember" that an uncle raped them when they were nine, but the remembering does not occur until age 49. This has caused quite a stir in affected families and in courtrooms. What are the statutes of limitation on a crime that took place 40 years ago?

Kimberly recently remembered that she was raped. She remembers it vividly and is certain of its truth. In fact, she describes remembering as a relief in some ways. "I always wondered why I was so depressed that I wanted to die. I knew something was at the core of it, and remembering this awful event has validated me on one hand." On the other, Kim says it has caused an unfamiliar strain in her physical relationship with her husband. "We always had a good sex life, and that, for now, is shattered. It makes me angry and it hurts me, but I'm glad to know that I had a reason for my deepest despair," Kim says.

Perhaps at the heart of the fray is the technique of the therapist. Kim was convinced something had happened to her long before she had a therapist who suspected the same. The approach of a therapist who immediately begins to suggest, "You have all the symptoms of someone who has been sexually abused. Do you recall such an incident or incidents?" could plant something in a desperate person's mind that was not there. On the other hand, a therapist who works with a patient over a significant period of time and begins to notice recurring references to people or places and symptoms of sexual abuse without prompting, might legitimately begin to explore this territory with their patient.

Recall Isabelle's dissociative safety valve that removed her from several incidents of childhood molestation, and her later dissociative disorder that prevented her from feeling pain even as she inflicted wounds on herself. Joan Beck reported in the *Chicago Tribune* that "Some events—like incest—may be so painful, so hard for the victim to understand, that a violated child copes by pretending they are happening to someone else or to some other self or even not happening at all. Eventually, the experiences become lost in the neuronal maze of memory in the brain and seemingly forgotten.

"But the repressed horrors can still take a psychological toll. In theory, forgotten sexual abuse can be the cause of emotional difficulties, depression, unhappiness, sexual problems, even multiple personality disorder.

"One study of 100 women with hospital records of sexual abuse as young children found that more than one-third of them could not remember it. Other research indicates that an even higher percentage of victims repress the memory of molestation at least at some times in their lives."

At the other side of the dilemma, "A growing number of people who have made bitter accusations—usually against relatives—have concluded they were misled by their therapists."[1]

Charlotte Hoffman is an Education Specialist (Ed.S.) and a Licensed Professional Counselor (LPC). She is in private practice in Madison, Alabama. Here, she further explains what repression is and how it functions.

Despite the skepticism of some colleagues in the mental health profession, Ms. Hoffman strongly believes in the mind's ability to repress traumatic events.

"It's a defense mechanism", she says. "Victims cannot deal with it [the violation and horror of the trauma]. The unconscious has a way of withholding information from us until we are strong enough to deal with it." [2]

☾ FAREWELL TO HIGHLAND

Since I wrote *Eclipses: Behind the Borderline Personality Disorder,* Highland Hospital in Asheville, North Carolina was closed as a psychiatric facility. Since then several of the DBT-trained psychiatrists and therapists who worked at that hospital have opened private practices in the Asheville area. Please refer to the "Who to Contact" listing (page 140) for information on where to find more information and professionals who believe in the success they have seen applying Dialectical Behavior Therapy in their treatment of patients with borderline personality disorder. The following editorial appeared in the *Asheville-Citizen Times,* and expresses my personal feelings about the hospital closing:

> How does one say goodbye to a hospital—one that has provided quality mental health care since 1904; one that taught me how to survive?
> Does one focus on the illustrious history, and more famous patients such as Zelda Fitzgerald? While

F. Scott Fitzgerald drank and stayed at the Grove Park Inn he was bullying to his ill wife during visitations. Zelda was doomed to perish in a fire in 1948 that claimed nine women's lives. Staff members recount how boys from the Montford community dove in and rescued several patients—I slept better during my three stays at Highland knowing that.

Does one focus on the groundbreaking programs in Dialectical Behavior Therapy begun by a Seattle psychologist but offered through Highland as one of the only other sites in the United States? This program teaches ways to prevent suicidal acts.

Or, does one mention the ugly politics of a corporate buyout based on "profitability" as Highland's personnel disperses—some following patients to Appalachian Hall [now Charter-Asheville]—dismantle programs and the campus goes up for sale?

I've learned to want to live again. It took three relatively long stays; it took tears and outbursts, escape attempts, suicide attempts, self-starvation and, at last, acceptance of the coping skills offered on a silver platter all those months by doctors, nurses, psychiatric assistants, activity therapists, cafeteria personnel, and God's own hand in the creation of the profuse rhododendron blossom and random acts of human kindness—you meet the nicest people in mental hospitals.

[To the new owner], please don't remove the billboard that states: "Life, Be In It."

❮ WHERE ARE ALL THE BOYS?

Highland Hospital's Borderline Personality Unit admitted a vast majority of female patients. In fact, approximately 79 percent of the community was female. Linehan also noted that the majority of her borderline patients were (and are) female. Dr. Eric Peterson theorizes that women may have more predisposition to biological emotional vulnerability from an early age.

"However, we have treated males diagnosed with borderline personality disorder," he recalls. "I believe that some of the discrepancy between the number of females and males so diagnosed might well have to do with how society perceives the acting out behavior often associated with it." In other words, when a female throws an uncontrollable tantrum, she might wind up in a therapist's office. Conversely, when a male feels these strong emotions, he may act them out differently—drinking heavily and driving fast, performing acts of vandalism or using illegal drugs. The result? More males in these situations wind up in juvenile detention or prison, depending upon their age.

"Perhaps we should re-examine our view of antisocial behavior—so often associated with males exhibiting this type of behavior. There may well be more male borderlines than we in the psychiatric community have recognized," Peterson concludes.

A pervasive pattern of instability of interpersonal relationships, self-image, and affects, and marked impulsivity beginning by early adulthood and present in a variety of contexts, as indicated by five (or more) of the following:

(1) frantic efforts to avoid real or imagined abandonment. Note: Do not include suicidal or self-mutilating behavior covered in Criterion 5.

(2) a pattern of unstable and intense interpersonal relationships characterized by alternating between extremes of idealization and devaluation

(3) identity disturbance: markedly and persistently unstable self-image or sense of self

(4) impulsivity in at least two areas that are potentially self-damaging (e.g., spending, sex, substance abuse, reckless driving, binge eating). Note: Do not include suicidal or self-mutilating behavior covered in Criterion 5.

(5) recurrent suicidal behavior, gestures, or threats, or self-mutilating behavior

(6) affective instability due to a marked reactivity of mood (e.g., intense episodic dysphoria, irritability, or anxiety usually lasting a few hours and only rarely more than a few days)

(7) chronic feelings of emptiness

(8) inappropriate, intense anger or difficulty controlling anger (e.g., frequent displays of temper, constant anger, recurrent physical fights)

(9) transient, stress-related paranoid ideation or severe dissociative symptoms

Reprinted with permission from the Diagnostic and Statistical Manual of Mental Disorder, Fourth Edition. Copyright ©1994 American Psychiatric Association.

ℭ GLOSSARY

Abandonment—To leave completely and finally; desert

Bootstrap Therapy—Seen as the answer to a borderline, depressed, or any mentally ill person as "just put a smile on your face, there is nothing really wrong with you", which is a terrible and stigmatizing misunderstanding of "therapy" for these individuals

BPD–Borderline Personality Disorder—Ascribed to emotionally desperate, self-destructive people; lies between neuroses and psychoses

Cheerleading—The applauding of either self or other(s) after successful passage through a difficult time, such as non-parasuicidal behavior or use of skilled behavior

Crisis Intervention—Literally stopping, by force if necessary, harmful actions

DBT–Dialectical Behavior Therapy —A form of therapy assisting BPDs to hold opposite thoughts in their mind at the same time, i.e. something can be good and bad simultaneously; in other words looking at both sides of the coin

DEAR MAN—A DBT acronym; it refers to the skill of asking for something using the Describe, Explain, Assert, Reinforce, Mindfully, Appear (confident), Negotiate frame work; used because most borderlines have poor self-esteem and difficulty in speaking up about their emotions and especially their needs

Dialectical—Looking at or interacting with opposing ideas, for example, good/bad

Domino Effect—The phenomenon that refers to one person's mood or behavior affecting the other patients' behavior, usually in a hospital ward or halfway house; includes behavior such as screaming, stomping, or more serious behavior such as parasuicide

ECT–Electro-Convulsive Therapy—A mild shock given to the brain administered by a psychiatrist under general anesthesia; used usually when medications fail to work well; this treatment is given in a series over a period of weeks and is often followed by short-term memory loss

Generalization—The ability to apply as many DBT skills as possible to the same or different difficult situations

Hierarchy of DBT—Safety first, treatment interfering behaviors, healthy lifestyle changes, skilled behavior

Impulsive—Often dangerous act in which one "jumps before she/he thinks"

Mindfulness—A core skill that teaches one to be in the moment, perhaps even thinking or saying aloud "I am safe" "I am doing the laundry" "My cat is rubbing my legs"— the key is that it is non-judgmental toward what is going on even if "It is raining outside"

Modules—The series of skills learned through DBT, including core skills, emotional regulation skills, distress tolerance, and safety plans and contracts

One-to-Ones—Scheduled time to discuss, usually with a PA the day's events and how they were handled; includes feedback from the PA

PA—Psychiatric Aide/Assistant

Parasuicide—Any unsuccessful attempt at suicide taken extremely seriously by the professional regardless of the severity of self-harm

Pharmo-Psychotherapy—The use of medications such as antidepressants and anti-anxiety drugs to assist an individual

Prompting events—Any incident that leads to a period of destabilization in an individual; can be anything from whether the weather is bad to a death in the family; usually discussed thoroughly with the individual's therapist

Protocol—Formal paper work and session in front of at least two professionals and a peer group after a parasuicidal incident that involves, explaining what lead up to the incident and making any repairs in relationships that have been hurt due to the fact that the individual did not ask for help beforehand

Psychiatrist—Medical doctor trained in psychological field; licensed to prescribe medication

Quiet room—A closely monitored room used for patients at risk; usually has only a made up mattress for sleeping comfortably and no furniture with which the individual could harm themselves

Reintegrate—Process of resuming control of one's life, gradual socialization

Safe place—An image an individual conjures up during difficult periods that helps calm them, such as a warm beach, clear mountains, a favorite chair or book—whatever works for them

Safety Plans/Contracts—A plan, normally placed on index or other small cards to be kept with an individual at all times upon discharge from treatment; includes what to do in prioritized order to keep them safe; might begin with mindfulness and end with calling 911; this is usually a contract between the patient and therapist or other(s) who understand and is highly successful in preventing self-harm

Splitting—The inability of borderlines to hold opposites in their mind simultaneously, such as good and bad, black and white, happy and sad; the inability to find a middle ground

Stabilization period—A short-term stay in a hospital for someone who has committed parasuicide or is at high risk for doing so, with medication adjustments as needed

Stigma—Mark of disgrace or infamy; negative reaction, a taboo

Stuffing—Keeping all emotions inside rather than venting appropriately when necessary for one's mental health

Suicide—Self-inflicted death

Support system—Multi-source of unconditional, effective help even in dire times

Therapist—Professional trained in some area of mental health, usually holds a Ph.D. or perhaps other degrees. Those with M.D.s are licensed to prescribe prescriptions

Turtling—A core skill taught to protect oneself; pull one's head in like a turtle

Unhealthy coping mechanisms—The way a borderline gets by, whether it be by cutting, stuffing, or other unhealthy behaviors; seen as such by professionals who nonetheless insist on and assist with change to healthy coping mechanisms

Validation—Approval, support of a person or person's situation, decision, etc.

Warm Ruthlessness—A phrase used by Marsha Linehan, Ph.D. developer of DBT; refers to admitting the patient is going through a difficult time but insisting on a change in behavior to prevent self-harm; also refers to seeking help before an incident of self-harm occur

Wellness—Solid mental health—mostly seen in BPDs who continue treatment

Wise Mind—DBT skill, using logical and emotional thought simultaneously

NOTES

Chapter 1
1 Linehan, *Skills Training Manual for Treating Border-line Personality Disorder,* p.1
2 William D. Barley, Ph.D., et al. "Development of an Inpatient Cognitive-Behavioral Treatment Program for Borderline Personality Disorder," Journal of Personality Disorders 7 (3), 1993
3 Linehan, *Skills Training Manual for Treating Border-line Personality Disorder,* p.4
Chapter 2
1 Linehan, *Skills Training Manual for Treating Border-line Personality Disorder,* p. 5
2 Linehan, *Skills Training Manual for Treating Border-line Personality Disorder,* p. 5
3 Linehan, *Skills Training Manual for Treating Border-line Personality Disorder,* p. 3
Chapter 6
1 Barley, et al, Journal of Personality Disorders 7[3], 1993)
Appendix A
1 Beck, The Huntsville (Alabama) Times, Dec. 5, 1993).
2 Hoffman, The Huntsville (Alabama) Times, January 16, 1994.

BIBLIOGRAPHY

BARLEY, William D., et al. "Development of an Inpatient Cognitive-Behavioral Treatment Program for Borderline Personality Disorder," Journal of Personality Disorders 7 (3), 1993)

CHANCE, Sue *Stronger Than Death*, (W W Norton & Co, New York,1992)

FRANKL, Viktor Emil *Man's Search for Meaning : An Introduction to Logotherapy*, (Beacon Press, Boston, 1992)

KAYSEN, Susanna *Girl, Interrupted*, (Vintage Books, New York, 1994)

KREISMAN, Jerold Jay and Hal Strauss *I Hate You—Don't Leave Me: Understanding the Borderline Personality* (Avon Books, New York, 1989)

LINEHAN, Marsha M. *Cognitive-Behavioral Treatment of Borderline Personality Disorder,* (Guilford Press, New York, 1993)

LINEHAN, Marsha M. *Skills Training Manual for Treating Borderline Personality Disorder* (Guilford Press, New York, 1993)

WHO TO CONTACT FOR MORE INFORMATION

Please note: the names and addresses were current at the time of printing but are subject to change without notice. On the World Wide Web, visit http://www.msano.com/eclipses.html for the latest information on these resources.

Specifically about Dialectical Behavior Therapy:
The following list is for informational purposes only. For more information on selecting a therapist, contact the American Psychiatric Association or the Amercian Psychological Association.

Dr. William Barley
The Pisgah Institute
P.O. Box 2035
Asheville, North Carolina 28802
(704) 254–9494

Dr. Eric Peterson and Dr. Beverly Brooks
Asheville, North Carolina
(704) 252–3375

Dr. Charles Swenson
Area Office, Department of Mental Health
Western Massachusetts
(413) 584–1644, ext. 341

Dr. Marsha M. Linehan
University of Washington, Department of Psychology
Box 351525
Seattle, Washington 98195–1525
(206) 685–2037

William Smalley, Ph.D.
Cedarcrest Regional Hospital
525 Russell Road
Newington, CT 06111
(860) 666–4613   (Inpatient DBT skills training)

George Davis, Ph.D.
Assistant Clinical Professor of Psychiatry
Yale New Haven Hospital
20 York Street
New Haven, CT 06504
(203)785–2117 Office of Psychiatry
(203) 785–4242 (general information)
(203) 787–3070 (psychiatry department)
(Inpatient and outpatient DBT training)

Tom Lynch, Ph.D. or Clive Robins, Ph.D.
Duke University Medical Center
P.O. Box 3362
Department of Psychiatry
Durham, NC 27710
(919) 684–5265   (Inpatient DBT skills training)

Resources on the World Wide Web:
http://members.aol.com/BPDCentral
Information on borderline personality disorder, including information on email discussion lists for borderlines and friends and families of borderlines.

http://www.apa.org/psychnet
American Psychological Association PsychNET®

http://www.psych.org
American Psychiatric Association

http://www.nami.org
National Alliance for the Mentally Ill

http://www.nmha.org
National Mental Health Association

If someone you love has borderline personality disorder:
An informative booklet is available, written especially for
friends and families of individuals with BPD. For more
information, call Randi Kreger at (888) 357–4355 (toll
free) in the US and Canada or (414) 454–9085

General Mental Health Resources:
American Psychiatric Association
1400 K Street, N.W.
Washington, D.C. 20005
(202) 682–6000

American Psychological Association
750 First St., N.E.
Washington, DC 20002–4242
(202) 336–5500

The Menninger Clinic
PO Box 829
Topeka, KS 66601-0829
(913) 350–5553 or (800) 351–9058

National Alliance for the Mentally Ill
200 North Glebe Road, Suite 1015
Arlington, Virginia 22203-3754
Toll Free Helpline (800) 950–NAMI (6264)
Front Desk (703) 524–7600

National Mental Health Association
1021 Prince Street
Alexandria, VA 22314-2971
(703) 684–7722
Mental Health Information Center (800) 969–NMHA

INDEX

A

abandonment 55, 81, 135
  fear of 10, 13
abuse 12, 19, 20, 27
acting out 133
alcohol abuse 20, 21
aloneness 1, 10, 22, 118
American Psychiatric Association
  24, 31
anger 98
anorexia nervosa 19, 27, 31, 79,
  80, 120
anti-anxiety drugs 136
antidepressant drugs 107, 136
antisocial behavior 133
anxiety 123
anxiety, antiolytics for 108
anxiety attacks 108

B

Barley, William xi, 7, 8, 9, 12,
  20, 28, 38, 74, 76, 80, 94,
  98, 106, 107, 123, 125,
  139, 140, 141
Bootstrap Therapy 115, 117,
  135
"borderline" as misleading term
  22
borderline personality disorder
  1, 22, 31, 87, 107, 135
  causes 20
  DBT as treatment 8, 74, 131
  depression and 107
  description 6
  males with 133

prognosis ix
self-harm 7
statistics viii, ix, 3
suicide and 7
suicide rate ix
symptoms 20, 134
borderlines
  and invalidating families 30
  as caregivers 102
  as perfectionists 25
  as survivor 96
  depression and 12
  friends and families of 112
  male 133
  prognosis of ix
  sexual abuse and 12
  splitting and 17, 135
  staying in therapy 123, 124
  suicide rate of ix
  validation and 28

C

Chance, Sue 57, 90, 92
cheerleading 104, 135
Cognitive-Behavioral Treatment...
  68, 140
Commitment (poem) 126
confidentiality 46, 102
coping mechanisms 6, 13, 24, 27,
  123, 138
crisis intervention 32, 70, 93, 99,
  109, 110, 135
cutting 19, 28, 61, 101, 138

D

DBT 43
DEAR MAN 84, 86, 135
DEAR MAN FAST 85, 86
DEAR MAN GIVE 85, 86
defense mechanism 130
depression 12, 20, 21, 23, 27,
    29, 30, 31, 48, 67, 71, 90,
    91, 105, 106, 107, 113,
    116, 119, 122, 129
dialectical 104, 110, 120, 135
Dialectical Behavior Therapy
    viii–ix, ix, 3, 4, 8, 9, 12, 13,
    24, 27, 28, 40, 64, 68, 69,
    70, 71, 72, 74, 75, 76, 87,
    88, 94, 100, 103, 131, 135
diary card (in DBT) 94, 95, 101
dissociation 20, 27
dissociative identity disorder *See*
    multiple personality
    disorder
Distress Tolerance 87, 88, 91,
    92, 94, 101, 136
Distress Tolerance skills
    distraction 88
    self-soothing 89
Domino Effect 45, 61, 102, 136
drug abuse 20, 21

E

eclipse 1, 2, 34, 93, 127
    about the title vi
Electro-Convulsive Therapy
    105, 106, 107, 113, 136
Emily 5, 9, 11, 12, 32, 38, 42,
    44, 46, 51, 58, 62, 65, 74,
    76, 116, 120, 123, 127,
    109, 115, 116, 124, 131,

Emotion Regulation Skills 79,
    80, 86
    Doing the Opposite 82
    Identify Obstacles to Chang-
        ing Emotions 80
    Increasing Mindfulness to
        Current Emotions 82
    Increasing Positive Emotional
        Events 81
    Reducing Vulnerability to
        "Emotion Mind" 81
emotions 2, 7, 9, 19, 23, 28, 29,
    31, 50, 58, 61, 79, 80, 86,
    88, 90, 96, 98, 120, 133,
    135, 138
    controlling 81
    difficulty controlling 13, 31
    myths about 59
    painful emotionality 6

F

Fitzgerald, F. Scott 132
Fitzgerald, Zelda 131
Frankl, Viktor Emil 69, 140

G

generalization 122, 136
Girl, Interrupted 16, 140
group therapy 40, 49, 60, 102,
    103, 111
    benefits of 102

H

Highland Hospital 8, 9, 27, 28,
    32, 33, 35, 38, 40, 41, 43,
    45, 47, 49, 50, 51, 52, 53,
    54, 57, 64, 74, 75, 76, 79,
    80, 90, 94, 95, 102, 105,

132, 133
hope vi, 12, 69, 70
hopelessness 67
hospitalization 4, 26, 40, 64, 66,
    70, 74, 75, 98, 108, 110,
    122, 123, 124
  life after 44, 64, 65, 124
  long-term care 32
  short-term care 33
hostility 108
How I Feel Today (poem) 118
hyper-sensitive 33

I

I Hate You–Don't Leave Me 3,
    22, 140
ice cubes
  as substitute for self-harm 9,
    28, 101
impulsive behavior 22, 76, 95,
    108
incest 129
Interpersonal Effectiveness Skills
    83, 86
invalidation 6
Isabelle 5, 9, 10, 11, 12, 15, 18,
    19, 20, 21, 22, 23, 27, 32,
    38, 42, 45, 46, 48, 51, 52,
    53, 57, 58, 69, 88, 92, 93,
    95, 96, 97, 106, 114, 119,
    120, 124, 125, 127, 129

K

Kaysen, Susanna 16, 18, 140
Keillor, Garrison 4
Kimberly 5, 12, 21, 23, 32, 45,
    58, 61, 62, 63, 81, 89, 92,
    100, 101, 105, 106, 107,
    113, 114, 122, 127, 128,
    129
Kreisman, Jerold Jay 140

L

laxatives, abuse of 124
Linehan, Marsha ix, 6, 8, 12,
    17, 20, 27, 30, 33, 43, 58,
    59, 68, 69, 70, 77, 79, 80,
    82, 84, 85, 87, 89, 91, 94,
    100, 104, 119, 124, 133,
    138, 139, 140, 141
loneliness 50, 67
loss 12, 15, 57, 71, 92, 104, 113

M

manipulative 23, 87
Man's Search for Meaning 69,
    140
medication 27, 60, 63, 99, 107,
    108, 109, 110, 112, 116,
    120, 121, 122, 123, 136,
    138
medications ix
Meichenbaum, Donald 76
MFT *See* Thornton, Melissa
    Ford
Mindfulness 78, 79, 82, 86, 88,
    123, 136, 137
mood instability 108
multiple personality disorder
    129

N

Negatron 55, 56, 58
New York Hospital's Cornell
    Westchester Division 8, 27,

37, 40, 43, 50, 69, 74, 75, 95

P

pain 6, 7, 10, 15, 18, 20, 22, 72,
    78, 89, 90, 91, 92, 93, 101,
    129
panic attacks 108
parasuicide 6, 7, 8, 46, 95, 136,
    138 *See also* self-harm
Peggy 5, 12, 21, 23, 29, 30, 32,
    45, 46, 48, 51, 58, 62, 63,
    82, 90, 91, 97, 105, 106,
    113, 114, 115, 127
Peterson, Eric 7, 8, 17, 20, 22,
    28, 44, 55, 63, 75, 89, 105,
    107, 133, 141
Peterson, Eric W. xi
Pharmo-Psychotherapy 136
Positron 55, 56, 58
post traumatic stress disorder 20,
    31, 71
prompting events 104, 137
Pros and Cons, skill of 94, 101
protocol 96, 97, 99, 137
pseudonyms vi
psychiatrist 23, 47, 108, 137
psychologist 23, 47
PTSD *See* post traumatic stress
    disorder

Q

quiet room 45, 46, 47, 51, 62,
    137

R

Rachel 67, 70, 74, 82, 118
rape 128
relief 2, 7, 8, 9, 19, 24, 28, 89,

92, 98, 101, 106, 107, 128
Remnants of a Childhood (poem)
    14
repressed memories 20, 128
repression 128, 130
rescue 7
revenge 7, 98

S

safety plans 98, 99, 136, 137
    contracts 99, 136, 137
self-harm 2, 7, 9, 13, 23, 24, 28,
    33, 62, 63, 82, 98, 136
    avoiding 51
    cause 2
    contracts 99, 100
    DBT hierarchy 40, 104
    Pros and Cons skill 94, 111
    protocol 95
    safety plans 137
    substitute for 89, 98, 101
    warm ruthlessness 138
self-mutilation 20 *See also* self-
    harm
self-respect 85, 86
sexual abuse 12, 13, 52, 128, 129
Skills Training Manual 59, 68,
    77, 139, 140
sleeplessness 108
Smothered (poem) 67
splitting 17, 19, 23, 27, 31, 37,
    137
stigma 24, 66, 88, 124, 135, 138
Strauss, Hal 140
Stronger Than Death 57, 90, 140
suicide 6, 7, 19, 21, 50, 61, 66,
    90, 91, 92, 113, 114, 116,
    132, 138

rate of, in borderlines 13
Swenson, Charles 43, 95, 141
symptoms 15, 20, 21, 31, 107,
    108, 134

T
testimonials 3, 69
Thornton, Melissa Ford vii, viii,
    x, 3, 4, 10, 14, 33, 34, 35,
    37, 57, 64, 73, 116, 124,
    126
trauma 20, 104, 105, 130
turtling 76, 99, 138

U
University of Washington, Seattle
    ix, 68

V
validation 29, 110, 112, 138
verbal abuse 18
vulnerability 6

W
warm ruthlessness 104, 138
wellness 33, 37, 113, 120, 138
Wise Mind 70, 76, 77, 78, 86,
    107, 138

The type in this book was set in:
Trajan (book title)
Adobe Garamond (text)
Avant Garde Book (diagrams)
Minion Expert Ornaments